WHEN IN DOUBT,
STEP ON THE GAS

Sophie Echeverria

Cover design and book layout by Rebecca Woods

Address correspondence to:
Sophie Echeverria
P.O. Box 546
Moulton Loop
Jackson, Wyoming 83001

WHEN IN DOUBT, STEP ON THE GAS

A RAGGED MEMOIR

by

SOPHIE ECHEVERRIA

Wickenburg, Arizona and
Jackson Hole, Wyoming

I write this hoping that it will

in some way honor

JACK AND SOPHIE BURDEN

To Whom it is dedicated

Acknowledgements

This small book of tall tales could not have happened without the wonderful help of friends and colleagues. My everlasting gratitude goes to Susanne Walsh, who can make my computer behave, and she made me "behave," organizing my chaotic efforts and editing. Great friends Ron Brownell, his sister Barbara and her partner Elayne Feldstein, helped with encouragement, editing and excellent insights—also fun in New York City.

My beloved daughters Elaine and Anne read early versions and provided insights I value. While my daughter Sophie has not read any of the book, she is a published author and is publishing another book, which she will not show me. The two of us have had great times moaning about writer's block and kicking each other in the backsides to keep us going.

The members of the Jackson Hole Writers Group have been consistently wise and helpful as well as a ton of fun. The Jackson Writers Conferences supplied critiques that shook me up and got me going in other directions. Zac Rosser's enthusiasm and wisdom urged me on. He has edited and printed out versions of the book with excellent ideas. Tim Sandlin has cheered me on and has edited the manuscript which resulted in yet another re-write.

For now, Thank you all, dear people! May the book justify your good help.

TABLE OF CONTENTS

PROLOGUE:
IT'S ALL IN THE DNA

The Domingo Echeverria family history is a tall tale, a seething stew of travail, tragedy and triumph. Any attempt to achieve historical accuracy is doomed as the story dances through time like something almost mythical and often hard to believe.

Unfortunately, or maybe fortunately, I am the one who has been elected to tell it. Cornelia Otis Skinner helpfully offers wisdom: "One learns in life to listen and to draw one's own confusions." I have listened, drawn mine, and obviously so has most everyone else. Where memory is concerned one's "confusions" are so subjective, so varied in what influenced them that we will sit around discussing an issue, each fervently believing their view is accurate, and after awhile we wonder if we are even talking about the same thing. Does truth where memories are concerned even exist? I submit to you, kind reader, what to me is true. Confusion is inevitable when one is skidding sideways toward a "distinguished age" stirring up clouds of dust, as I am, with contributions from my astonishingly confused family. Even amidst all our subjective ambiguities we rejoice, by God. Let us begin.

Paul Echeverria, thirty-five, bright and good-looking, got roaring drunk at a wild party up in the mountains near Aspen, Colorado. Blazing down the mountain in his Blazer he careened around a curve, plunged off a cliff and landed upside down in a stream. Thrown from the vehicle, there was my wonderful son, unconscious, with his head under water. He would have drowned had his friend Spencer not been conscious enough, though injured, to hold Paul's head up until someone heard his frantic calls for help.

Spencer was hospitalized in Glenwood Springs down the valley from Aspen, but Paul needed intensive care beyond their capability. Though essentially unconscious he was so violent it took five policemen to get him restrained and into a helicopter to be flown to St. Mary's Hospital in Grand Junction. He slid into deep unconsciousness and lay, tied down, for four and a half days. His wife June, his little children Charlie Anne and Jack, and his two brothers and three sisters gathered from near and far as it looked as if we might lose him. I called two doctor friends to ask if we should fly him to Denver or Phoenix for better care. Both called back saying that a blessing was ours. One of the nation's leading brain specialists had recently left his practice in Los Angeles to raise his children in Grand Junction and he would be Paul's doctor.

Dr. Tice said, "Sophie, you must accept the fact that when Paul comes to, he will be different." To which I replied, "God, I hope so." So handsome, charming, and huge- of- heart, Paul had nonetheless terrified me for years with his wild behavior.

Dr. Tice told us much about head trauma and what happens to the brain when it suffers an injury like Paul's, spellbinding information. The human brain is beyond comprehension, surely enmeshed with God, gorgeous and terrifying in complexity and mystery. He told us that sometimes people regain consciousness speaking a foreign language. "Norphasic language disturbance" is its medical name and it happens, though rarely, following closed brain trauma. A teen-aged son of local ranchers awoke speaking French, which he could not possibly have known how to speak. A nun, one of Paul's nurses, told of two priests who had revealed far more in foreign languages, than anyone wanted to know upon awakening from head injuries. She wondered if their holy vocations had been chosen to overcome those shadowy sides. It made us wonder with apprehension what Paul would be like.

Dr. Tice, some books on psychology and on the mystical/spiritual aspects of our minds that I read after Paul's crash, put forth the belief that people who relive past lives under hypnosis or during therapeutic regressions strongly support the theory that much of who we are is in our DNA, and that DNA is carried down from generation to generation. The spiritual writers see it as Karma, perhaps another way of talking about DNA. Harvard University did a study that indicated almost 70% of behavior is in our DNA. Holy Moses, it is not all our fault after all! Or is it?

It was my turn to stand watch beside Paul. Suddenly he opened his eyes. "Paul, you're back!" I exclaimed. Most uncharacteristically for someone as "cool" as he was, he replied, "Yeah, Jesus sent me back.

He said there was something I had to do." Then he went stark raving bananas.

A Japanese Samurai warrior was his new identity, and he saw me as the Grand Matriarch of The Lion Clan. He bounded around his Craig Bed, a big, padded pen, doing karate moves, his Samurai yells bouncing off the hospital walls. After a few days, he said, "Mom, you have to get me out of here! You think this place is run by a bunch of holy nuns. Those black robes are just a cover. They are really running St. Mary's as a whore house!" "Good God, Paul, how did you come up with that?" I asked. He could see out the second story window which overlooked the hospital entrance, and he had been watching people come and go. Indignantly he said, "Can't you see it? Everyone leaving here's smiling. That's proof!" St. Mary's decided to move him to a rehabilitation facility where he slowly began to recover. After three or four months there he was sent home, but it took three scary years before he could function well enough to be trusted. He did things like forget he was in charge of his children while June worked and he would simply go off without them. He couldn't remember their names and called them "Short" and "Shorter." But he was indeed changed, kinder and more aware, and his life is better in spite of his confusion. He has a mission. In his own way, quietly, or sometimes not so quietly, he rescues people who are sinking. His lovely home was often a port in a storm for his drunk and druggy friends. He is a healer.

What else, besides the Japanese Lion Clan, lies in our family's DNA? What have our ancestors passed down to us to contribute to who we have become? I dove into research, combed the family history on both my side and my husband's. Plenty turned up that explains at least partly why we are the way we are; contrarians, rebels, but essentially quite nice.

A Ragged Beginning

Peregrin White was aboard the Mayflower, escaping persecution of some kind in merry old England, when it landed at Plymouth Rock, the first ship to come to North America. (There are claims that Vikings and Basques got there first, credibly substantiated by artifacts archeologists have uncovered). Or was he on that difficult voyage fired with adventure, in search of a new life? Another version of his history had it that he was born on the Mayflower, which must have been perfectly awful. Whatever, there he was among the Pilgrims and the Native American Indians, friendly until they started murdering each other, forging a new life in a new land. Beyond that, little is known about him other than that he sired twenty-one children, some of whom were our ancestors.

Clementine Fletcher, my maternal grandmother, did the genealogical research. How delighted she was to find us descended from the Mayflower itself! Peregrin was a source of pride unsullied by the possibility that all those children might indicate something other than Puritanical propriety. Clem, nicknamed "The Bird Lady" for her slight build and twittering personality, was one to relish the good and to ignore what did not please her, a wise skill if one can pull it off. She often quoted the Fletcher Motto: "Hoping, we go on." And on she went. Whatever Peregrin's excesses, his legacy turned out to be impressive. The first governor of Rhode Island was married to a Dexter, our ancestor, and Clem discovered others of the twenty-one children who rose to produce prestige and wealth. If she found out about the ones who did not, she didn't tell.

Thomas Fletcher made it over from England in 1792. A skilled weaver, he was forbidden to bring his loom, as England jealously guarded the industry that so enriched her government. Thomas, bright and brave, memorized how to build the loom and how to weave on it. Somehow he escaped with those pirated skills to join his family, Peregrin's descendents, in New England. They prospered making lamp wicks until electricity was brought in, when they segued to weaving the hair ribbons that adorned the elaborate wigs men of importance wore. Women needed corset laces to cinch them up to the prized eighteen-inch "wasp waists" so Tom and company cranked them out. He also invented grommets, those little metal rings around lacing holes, a small but universal invention which added to Clem's cache of pride and is a little piece of trivia that might be prized by anyone who is into very little pieces of trivia.

Business thrived and was expanded into woolen mills. By the time my great grandparents were born, an empire had been created, controlling wool and textile markets throughout New England. Their factories and warehouses lined the Moshassuck, a tributary to the Providence River. The Fletcher Building, their headquarters, was the

14

tallest in Providence for many years. William Fletcher extended trade to New York, where he lived in a penthouse atop the Waldorf Astoria. Back in Rhode Island, Tom, Joseph and John Fletcher diversified into real estate, and Fletcher Reality grew to control swatches of valuable property in and around Providence. Peregrin's daring ambition was trickling down in the family DNA quite splendidly.

Meanwhile, Down South

New Bern, North Carolina, was home to the Whitfords, our southern ancestors. The head of the clan, John D. Whitford, was an early and important member of the Masons, a founder of the Atlantic and North Carolina Railroad Company, and the Mayor of New Bern. The accomplishments achieved under his offices in the Masons and the State were so respected that a pile of silver dollars was melted down, made into a punch pitcher and presented to him with fanfare. The Ordinance of Secession that began the Civil War was partly his doing, and he fought with distinction enough to gain the rank of Colonel. The family seems to have clung to the old Confederate beliefs, and they have talked about "The problem of the blacks" right on down to my Grandmother's generation.

Colonel Whitford's son, William, did as so many sons of distinguished fathers do. He became a raging alcoholic, but not before he managed to marry Sophie Cordelia Stevenson. As usually happens when alcoholism sloshes into the picture, the family was financially strapped and in perpetual turmoil. Humor and dogged perseverance saved them in the tradition of the family's beloved icon, Don Quixote, famous for jousting with windmills. They survived with something like his beguiling wit and charm as they jousted away with ever threatening disaster. My grandmother Clementine, the "Bird Lady," played the guitar and sang songs racy enough to attract a merry following. She also taught dancing to add to the family income. It was said not a lot was learned but they had plenty of fun.

Parties were noisy with laughter and shouts as they competed at cards, croquet and whatever they could devise. Clem said of her mother, Sophie Cordelia, "She was a 'caution.' She was a marvelous croquet player, but she cheated." That wasn't all she did. The upstairs was rented out to provide much needed income, and when the renters pounded on their floor about the racket downstairs, Sophie Cordelia pounded the ceiling with her cane and yelled right back.

"Miss Delia," as she was called, was an imposing lady, dignified (in her own way) and imperious, proud of her noble heritage. Her ancestry was traced back to the DeChapotin family in the French Revolution. They were high enough in King Louis and Marie Antoinette's court to be in peril, destined for the guillotine along with the royals. They escaped, legend has it, by crawling down a ditch in the dead of night to the coast, where they caught a ship bound for North Carolina. They must have been good at crawling, as they arrived with the family coat of arms and plenty of money, perhaps tucked into their bustles.

A proud tradition was created to honor them, and each generation was to have a Sophie and a Clementine, and so it has been until

16

now. The Western song, "My Darlin' Clementine, whose shoes were boxes without topses because her feet were number nine"—kind of took the shine off the nobility and the name Clementine is used no more. Maybe a dog will turn up named Clem. There have been several Sophie dogs and so many girls named Sophie, including me, that it has become confusing.

Captain Pearce sailed the ocean blue but he must have been on land some, as he managed to capture lovely Clementine de Chapotin with whom he produced nine children. Sophie Cordelia, the "caution" that was my grandmother Clementine's mother was one of them. She was swept off her feet by Mr. Whitford, of Brown University in Rhode Island, and married him in spite of his heavy drinking. They moved to New Bern and began their family. "Papa Doolie" as he was called, and "Miss Delia" had two daughters. Sophie, beautiful, blonde and famously stylish, became an alcoholic and died in an institution. She had a son, also alcoholic who died of that dreadful malady. Clementine, our grandmother, was bright and courageous enough to rise above family problems.

She was a great shot, among other things. Alligators sometimes swam up the inlet near their home, and Clem, all five feet three of her in her in wasp-waisted, flowery finery, large hat perched on her shiny brown hair, took rifle in hand and marched down to the shore. She swept the murky surface with her gun until she had a bead on a threatening critter and BOOM! It was dispatched. She was famous not only for that but for her vivacious beauty, and a yacht was named after her.

17

The Clementine proudly sailed the North Carolina coast in her honor.

Papa Doolie's brother, Uncle Johnny Whitford, added to the family "excitement." He was an engineer on the very railroad created and run by his famous father, with a route up and down the East coast. When he died, two bereaved families turned up, one from each end of his run, with numerous children. It was quite a shock all around.

To the North We Go

The Fletchers had become died-in-the-wool (most of which they owned) New England business moguls in the 1800 and 1900's. One of the textile barons produced my great grandmother on my mother's side, Belvedere Fletcher, a "famous beauty," as beautiful women were called then. There was an oil portrait of her, the paint cracked with age, which I asked the Fletchers if I could buy, as she looked so much like my daughter Elaine. They would have none of it, jealously tight as they were, and the painting has disappeared. It showed Belle with lively, dark eyes fringed with thick lashes. Her eyebrows arched dramatically, a mane of black hair framed her lovely face and her figure was deliciously hourglass. Her schooling was impeccable, at one of Providence's elite institutions for young ladies. They poured tea and read things suitable for young virgins. She was protected from boys until her debut at sixteen, and then they came courting. Her parents hoped for a prestigious match, but Belle was not about to settle down. She swanned about Providence in her phaeton pulled by her pair of black horses, also famous beauties. In her wake languished young bachelors, but, as is often the way of beautiful girls, she tossed them to the wind. The Fletchers began to worry. She was eighteen and soon to be an old maid.

Along came Robert Lilly, "suitably connected" (As the rich were tactfully called), and oozing charm. Their courtship was swift and frothy, drenched in champagne and alight with their laughter as they danced away the nights at Providence parties. They galloped around town on their splendid horses, played tennis, and sailed. They were married, the bride magnificent in flowing white, in St. Martin's Episcopal Cathedral. Their entrance into the Providence social whirl followed their honeymoon.

Belle's parents were so relieved to finally have their wild one settle down that they ignored the red flags her new husband occasionally flashed. There was something amiss about Robert and the marriage was troubled, but even so, they managed to produce first Edith, and then Prescott. The family history turns dark and secret at this point and little has been passed down. There was a scandalous divorce. Robert had deteriorated. "He went blind and sold umbrellas on the Providence town square," is all that has been told. Was he a bounder who bounded from bed to bed, catching syphilis along the way with its resulting blindness and insanity? Angry and scandalized, Belvedere reclaimed her maiden name. Young Prescott, ashamed and furious, changed his name to William Fletcher after his uncle who lived in the penthouse atop the Waldorf Astoria in New York.

Free again, Belvedere cruised about in her phaeton, drawn by her beautiful black horses with her two little children beside her, a glamorous divorcee. Eventually she remarried a jolly Irishman, "Foxy Grandpa," and happiness was hers and theirs.

Edith, aristocratic to the bone, with a biting wit and elegant looks, became an actress. She was so talented she dominated the Providence Play House Theater and her fame might have been even greater if it had not been "unseemly" for girls of her class to act on the professional stage. Which ever Webster created Webster's Dictionary had a nephew beguiling enough to capture her butterfly self, marry her and settle her into a fine house on the Brown University campus where she lived until she died. He held a position at the University, and with their connections they created glittering salons. Professors, theater people and the prominent of Providence gathered to drink prohibition liquor and fill the air with electric, rarified and often outrageous talk.

Only one child, little Helen, was produced, probably unplanned. Parties and theater events in Newport and New York kept them circulating to the best hotels or as houseguests in fine homes. They bragged about leaving little Helen in dresser drawers, quite the sophisticated and funny thing to do they thought. She grew up hating her parents and small wonder. Filled with their strange ideas about life she turned out to be "unique."

Eccentric and opinionated, she was yet another "caution" in a family rife with difficult characters. She married an architect as lacking in charm as she was. He was responsible for many of the ugly brick post offices across America. They had one daughter, Emily. Following "tradition," they left her in hotel bureau drawers as they partied away. Helen paid little attention to Emily, leaving her essentially abandoned as she grew up. Helen's cruelty took on more subtle impositions as she made angry and outrageous statements about politics, religion and society and as she blasted people with snide gossip. Such alarming and embarrassing weirdness earned Emily's hate, just as Edith had earned Helen's. Edith, perhaps hoping to make up for her failure as a mother, (or just to annoy Helen) was wonderful to Emily and Em loved her. Edith's kindness and her example of good manners and civility guided little Emily well and she grew up to be a lovely young lady.

Emily and I went to Lincoln, in Providence, the private boarding school previous family ladies had attended. We were close, mischievous cousins, and one of our favorite pastimes was to dig around in her Grandmother Edith's attic. Glorious spangled gowns, feather boas, be-jeweled high heeled shoes, ropes of pearls and outrageous hats immersed us in glamour as we paraded around the attic pretending to be famous actresses, splendidly awash in it all.

Sometimes Edith invited us to join her parties if her guests would tolerate teen-aged girls. She offered us cocktails which she poured copiously for everyone. As she aged, she lost her sight and stuck her fingers in the glasses as she poured to feel if they were full. Those fingers were also used to feel her way through everything else and it seemed we might catch leprosy or something, so we stayed sober and often hungry. Her guests survived, probably bolstered by all those drinks loaded with antiseptic alcohol.

Among her guests were young Brown University boys, and Emily and I had crushes on all of them. They tolerated us. What excitement for our naïve little selves!

Much later, Emily joyfully broke the family traditions of elegance and propriety and divorced her first husband, a proper sort of fellow, left her five children who mystified her, and took up with a chef. They married, or perhaps they did not, and operated various restaurants. He cooked, she waited tables. What a blow to Edith and Helen. Take that, you society bitches!

William II Took Another Road

Edith's brother, Belle's beloved son William, was a true genius. He looked like a genius. Wild, thick black hair, impressively bushy eyebrows, piercing eyes, and a ruggedly handsome face announced that here was someone who demanded attention. His brilliance was intimidating and he flashed a dry wit that was hilarious but sometimes hurtful. "And what makes you think THAT?" he would ask, and there his victim was, challenged to wonder why in the world he did think whatever it was. Painful, but an excellent teacher, he demanded that we consider what went on in our heads instead of just charging along thoughtlessly.

William graduated from Harvard Medical School when he was 17, Summa Cum Laude, the youngest ever to scale such a height. Belle was thrilled with her Son-the-Doctor, and he continued to practice until she died. The day of her death, he closed his office, saying, "Never again do I want to tell anyone the kind of sad news doctors have to convey. It meant so much to my mother, but now she is gone." His wit may have been cruel, but underneath, his heart was large and kind. He joined the Fletcher real estate business, holding court from his tenth floor corner office in the Fletcher Building.

Alligators Were Not Clem's Only Prey

Clem, a true Southern Belle, even as part of such a scandalous family, was invited to visit her grandfather, Leon Stevenson in Providence. His son was there with a friend from Harvard Medical School, the young Dr. William Fletcher himself. Slim and lithe, with those piercing, dark eyes and spectacular eyebrows, he was an imposing presence. When his intensity and Clem's sparkling charm bumped into each other electricity crackled and love bloomed.

Clem had to return home and William's young medical practice was so busy he could not follow her. They began a correspondence that led eventually to his proposal of marriage, two years later, by mail, and her acceptance, also by mail. The Old Dominion Steamship line had a route between Providence and New Bern so young Dr. Fletcher set sail, or "set steam," to collect his fiancé. She said she was afraid she would not recognize him since she had seen him only once two years before, but bravely she arrived at the pier, and there he was, unmistakable with his mane of black hair and his impressive eyebrows. Soon they were wed.

They lived in Providence from then on, a prosperous and proper life. Dr. Fletcher bought one of the first automobiles in Providence, a Stanley Steamer. Family and friends gathered to witness the grand launch. The tale has been told until it has become legend, passed down to this very day. William in a long duster and Clem in her flowered hat and dress enthroned themselves in the fine leather seats. Proudly they took off. All went well as they cruised past Brown University, but then College Avenue began to slope steeply toward the Providence River. They started down well enough, but the good doctor got confused and pressed the gas pedal instead of the brake as faster and faster they went, Clem yelling, "The brake, you fool! The brake!" They were headed for destruction but somehow William steered into a big hedge where the car sputtered to a halt. He got out, lent his hand to his furious wife and walked away from that cursed car forever. They never owned another one.

Children began arriving. It seems likely the young Fletchers expected to follow tasteful family tradition and have only two children. They forever teetered on the brink of perfection. William Fletcher IV and Clementine were ideal; handsome and lovely, and hopefully bright. William graduated from Brown University and joined the Fletcher real estate business. Clementine was trained to enchant, dressed in ruffles and frills, her blonde hair arranged in cascading ringlets. She studied ballet in New York City and was often asked to dance at garden parties.

Then Sophie arrived, surely unplanned and perhaps unwanted. Young Clementine's "princess hood" was threatened by her little sister's dark good looks and intelligence. Their mother coped by proclaiming, "Clementine is such a beautiful child! Sophie is rather plain and should be dressed in sailor middies and her impossible hair must be bobbed."

When Sophie was two, John Dexter was born on Easter day, affording him the nickname of "Peter Rabbit," which stayed with him except for the Rabbit. Small and delicate, he was no threat to William or to anyone. He was simply discarded, drifting through childhood, ignored except to be picked on. Sophie, with innate kindness, defended little Pete, even lying on top of him to take the blows of bullies, including those of their older siblings. Sophie, with her large and generous heart, continued to take care of him one way or another all their lives. Somehow, in spite of all that, Pete grew up to be one of the funniest people we knew. He was a pure delight.

After Pete's birth Clem banned Dr. Fletcher from her bed and they kept separate rooms and somewhat separate lives from then on. Birth control was non-existent, at least to them, but that may not have been the whole problem. (He snored so thunderously that my brothers and I used to charge our friends nickels to hear him while hiding under his bedroom window.) For all that, they remained together in a unique kind of partnership. On their fiftieth wedding anniversary he toasted her with champagne, saying, "Here's to fifty years with the wrong woman!" Everyone laughed, of course, but he may have been dead serious.

Dr. Fletcher was determined to raise his children, even little

Pete, to be strong, self sufficient and resilient, capable of meeting all challenges with grace and courage. To this end he sent them to camps. Sophie, my mother, swam like a dolphin, gracefully outstripping everyone with her long, fluid strokes. Her horsemanship was just as impressive. She won trophies—a source of pride for her parents. But then she was thrown from a horse and seriously injured. As she was rushed to the hospital for surgery her father commanded, "Do not cry, thoroughbreds do not cry, and you had better be a thoroughbred."

She passed that command on to my brothers and me. A terrible thing, as often when tears would be appropriate and healthy, there we stand, frozen, like ice. Just as she was. The only time we ever saw our mother cry was when her dog Woof, and her horse Ronnie, died. In the face of family deaths and disasters she maintained her stiff upper lip, a thoroughbred to the end. Perhaps her beloved animals, closer to her than any of us managed to be, were in another realm, and in that other place, she was free to cry.

Dr. Fletcher decided they had had enough of organized camps and devised his own. He took them to the Canadian wilderness for pack trips that lasted six weeks. The children were ordered to dive into glacial pools and swim among the chunks of ice. They scaled cliffs, climbed mountains and indeed became tough and adventurous. Except perhaps Clementine, who later pursued a softer life and married Jimmy, a society boy, who lost his mind and her. Another family scandal that has been kept a secret.

As summer waned and it was time to head back to civilization, they loaded their packhorses, mounted up and headed out. Dr. Fletcher got lost. Too embarrassed to admit it, he led them on; silently hoping they were going in the right direction. All day and into the black night they rode, trusting their horses not to step off any cliffs. Suddenly, far ahead, they saw a light. Dr. Fletcher exclaimed, "Look! A lout in a hise!" (A light in a house.) They were saved.

The Fletchers had inherited a genetic speech defect which produces "louts in hises" and other Spoonerisms. The Reverend Spooner himself was a distant ancestor and was so notorious for his slips that his name was given to the disorder. English, an albino and very small, he was none the less charming and well liked. He graduated from Oxford, became a lecturer on divinity, ancient history and philosophy, and was soon elevated to Dean. Eventually he became a priest in the Church of England, delightfully famous for his rearrangements of words. He sermonized about God, saying, "Our Lord is a shoving leopard." The Queen fared no better when he called her, "that queer old dean." After World War I he proclaimed, "When the boys come home we will have all the hags flung out!" He was most famous for a sermon about the Prodigal Son. He told of the father's joy at his son's return, and how, "in celebration, he killed a fatted calf and prepared a grand feast. As the son approached, the father ran to greet him and put a thing on his ringer." The tendency to produce Spoonerisms has been passed right on down to us, thank goodness. They go so well with our confusions.

Dr. Fletcher had a hard time maintaining his dignity. Southern to the end, Clem was a fierce Democrat. Northern all his life, he was a stubborn Republican. They never voted because, they said, they would just cancel each other out. Their fights about it were hardly civil. In exasperation, Clem would yell, "You are just Northern Scum!" Their children thought it was hilarious and began calling their father "Scummy." When they moved to Arizona, it was given a sort of Spanish spin and he became "El Scumpso" for the rest of his life. Those were the ancestors who produced my mother Sophie, who became one of the great western originals and who produced us, also quite original.

Top photo: William Fletcher as a young boy and left, as a young man. William, the author's maternal grandfather, was called "scum" by his wife, Clementine, for his staunch Republican views. The nickname morphed into "El Scumpso" when the family moved to Arizona. Widely recognized as a genius, William graduated Harvard Medical School at age 17.

Left photo: Sophie Cordelia Whitford, circa 1900. Sophie was mother to Clementine Steven-son Whitford, the author's maternal grandmother pictured in the photo to the right. Clemen-tine—affectionately called Nano by the author—married William Fletcher.

THE EARLY YEARS

INTO THE WIND

~

Our little helicopter climbed above Arizona's Bradshaw Mountains and circled toward Seal Peak. Far below we could see the Hassayampa River winding through its steep canyons. Sun flashed briefly on a pond, a sparkling jewel in the dry Arizona desert. "This is the place!" I shouted above the noise of the whirling rotors. Then we took turns, my brother John and I, throwing our brother Dana's ashes to the wind to float down to the land he so dearly loved. He had explored it until he knew intimately every boulder outcropping, every Saguaro, and every Mesquite and Palo Verde thicket.

Dana had died too soon, too young, of brain cancer. Slowly he slipped away from us. The tumor was inoperable, and he was told he would not survive more than six months even with full treatment. He chose to fight, and fight he did, undergoing radiation with a cheerfulness that charmed the technicians. His flirting and joking with nurses in the face of his inevitable death seemed almost strange, but it was also inspiring. The cheer became less and less as his brain was invaded. Hallucinations began. One morning he told us to warn everyone not to cross the river as it was in full flood, a rather nice delusion, actually. Dana's friends rallied around. Several times he fell, and John, with his bad back, couldn't lift him. We called the KL Bar Ranch, where Dana had given lectures to guests about area history, and asked the cowboys to come help. With obvious love for their friend, they were there in minutes to lift him gently into his bed.

His caretakers appeared almost magically, they were so perfect. Dana loved women. Tammy was expert at the kind of care he needed, and she was a vision to gladden his, and anyone else's, heart. Built like a Playboy Bunny, she appeared one morning in a tight t-shirt. Emblazoned across her splendid frontage was, "I'm not just a pretty face." Amen.

Six months after the diagnosis, he revived from the semi-conscious state he had fallen into and said, "George Hershkowitz came to visit! Fun to talk to him." George, a good, old friend, had died about two weeks earlier. Dana slipped into a coma. How good it was to know George, and surely others, were waiting to greet him. Tammy called before dawn on February 24, 2006, and said, "Come. It is time." I sped to Dana's beloved little home out on the desert where he had chosen to spend the final days of this hard time. Tammy and I sat on either side of him, holding his hands, as he took off for The Ultimate Adventure, the Great Leap. Tammy said, "I think I may have given him too much morphine. He was having a bad time." "Tammy," I said, hugging her, "How could there be too much morphine for someone who is dying and in distress? Thank God for it, and thank God for you."

He had told us, "I want my ashes to go back into the land.

Sprinkle me in the Bradshaws." And so we did, silently saying, "Fly, Dana, fly on the wind into the wild land where you had so many adventures. And thank you for taking us on so many of them."

The helicopter circled back, over Remuda Ranch just west of the mountains, where we had grown up. There it lay below us, a complex of beautiful, low buildings embraced by trees, lawns, and surrounded by desert, the place our parents had built with their own hands. The swimming pool our Dad had proudly created, shaped like a grand piano, was gone, replaced by another, sparkling in the sunshine. Some of the cottages we had loved had been razed and new buildings had been added. It had changed, but it was still Remuda Ranch, now a center for the treatment of bulimia and anorexia. It is a healing place, a place that does much good, and we are glad about that. It seems a fine transition from the guest ranch we had known, wildly western and riotously fun, more about outrageous behavior than about healing anything—except boredom.

Jack Burden

Our father, John Dana Burden, called Jack, was born and raised on Beacon Street, a fine address in Boston. His father, Dr. Ernest Burden, was a graduate of Harvard Medical School. His offices were on the ground floor of an imposing red, brick building across the street from a small park. His wife, Ellen Kate, their daughter Kate and son Jack lived in the top floor apartment. Their lives seemed to be nearly perfect, but there was mischief afoot.

Ellen Kate Robinson was the daughter of a sea captain who "sailed the ocean blue," just as Captain Pearce, our Southern ancestor had. His wife and daughter, their only child, were abandoned for months, sometimes years. Surely it was difficult, and no telling how it was for little Ellen Kate. Whatever her childhood challenges were, she emerged a paradox. She shimmered with finishing school charm, with the sophistication of Boston society, but underneath the sheen, fury festered. She grew up to be tall, and rather handsome, with what was then called "an aristocratic nose"—it looked like a witch's beak to me. That fury slithered out as she skewered us so subtly, so elegantly with her damning velvet needle comments we didn't even know we had been skewered until we began to feel awful. Jack escaped her fury because he was her idolized son, destined for greatness. But little Kate did not, and she grew up to be a beautiful, rebellious, red headed vixen.

Jack was a junior at Phillips Exeter Academy when rheumatic fever struck him down, crushing his brilliance and athletic ability. He had to leave school. The tragedy of his illness apparently brought years of discord to a head, and, in spite of scandal, Ellen Kate and Ernest divorced. She gathered up Jack and Kate, abandoned Boston and left for Arizona. When they arrived in Phoenix, Jack was taken from the train on a stretcher, his heart severely damaged.

Lies and Enterprise

Somehow, they found Wickenburg, a little ranching and mining town, 60 miles northwest of Phoenix. In 1924, not much was going on in that wild country, but they were told of rooms at Leo Weaver's Circle Flying W Cattle Ranch in the foothills east of town and they gratefully rented them. Bob White from Washington, D.C was there, also recovering from something and the two young men became friends as the warm sun and fresh air slowly healed them. When the summer heat set in, shimmering in waves across the desert, hitting triple digits on the thermometer, roasting their East Coast bones, they all moved to Prescott, higher and cooler.

The two young men, regaining health and feeling pretty lively, hung out in the bars along Prescott's infamous Whiskey Row, pretending to be ranchers and cowboys. They bought boots, Levis and Stetsons, in hopes of fitting in with the cowboys who were bellying up to the bars. The talk was about favorite horses, cattle, range conditions and ranch affairs. One day Jack asked who owned the string of good-looking horses he had seen along the road. He was told they were the remuda of a nearby cow outfit. "Remuda?" He asked. "Yeah, that is what the Mexican settlers called the strings of horses they rode to herd their cattle." Later, with mischief twinkling in their eyes, some locals asked the two young fellows pretending to be cowboys about the ranch they said they had. "What's it called?" Thinking fast, Jack said, "Why, Remuda. Yes, Remuda Ranch." Probably no one was fooled, but Jack and Bob were good looking and funny, so they were accepted as they were. They realized that they had better get that ranch and make honest cowboys of themselves.

As any sensible young Boston Brahmin and his East Coast

buddy would, they decided a guest ranch would be the very thing, since they didn't know the back end from the front of a cow, or what made a bull a steer, for goodness sake. They began to look for a place that would work. They were told about a property south of Wickenburg that sounded good.

The old Bar FX Ranch belonged to the O'Brien family, whose lives played out like country music dramas. The O'Briens had been in Wickenburg for generations, struggling to survive by prospecting for gold, hard-scrabble ranching, and taking in a few guests. When Jack drove up in his big, black phaeton with mother Burden, resplendent in flowery finery topped off with a large hat, and his sister Kate; delectable in jodhpurs and boots, her red mane somewhat in check under her Stetson, old lady O'Brien, widow of FX, thought for sure her ship had come in.

She invited them in, sat them down, rubbing her leathery hands with glee. Bob soon arrived and the coffee came, laced with something that made their throats tingle and their brains jingle. Jack looked around, assessing the prospects. Adobe, rock fireplaces, hand-hewn beams and tile floors, everything enhanced with the patina of age, created a rustic charm. The kitchen would never pass state inspection now, but back in the 1920s, no one cared about such trivia, and surely good meals could be produced on the big, wood-burning stove. The dining and living rooms needed better furniture and some Navajo rugs, but they were open and airy. The windows looked out on sub-irrigated pastures of Bermuda grass, bordered by the Hassayampa River on one side, and Turtleback Mountain and its surround of hills on the other. The house was embraced by bougainvillea, big mesquites, rows of stately palms, eucalyptus and grand old cottonwood trees. There were lots of flowers. It would definitely do.

There were nine bedrooms, and one outside bath. Jack and Bob planned to set up some little tent houses that were typically used to house patients suffering from tuberculosis who came to the desert to be cured. With good beds, linens, and rugs, the tents would be delightful and provide enough guest capacity to make a go of it.

Mrs. O'Brien lived on the edge when it came to gracious hostessing, and there was nothing in the way of decent linens or tableware. Jack and Bob's heads were whirring with mental lists of what they would need, but they didn't let on to Mrs. O. They just sat there with her, fondling their mugs of coffee-plus, letting her think they were as dumb as Westerners fancy Easterners to be. (Mutual.) A two-year lease with an option to buy was negotiated at the handsome sum of $25 per month. They shook on it, and Jack and Bob were honestly ranchers. Jack headed to Phoenix to do some research.

Phoenix's Chamber of Commerce was the place to learn how to run such a place, and how to lure guests. (One of the first things decided was to call it a guest ranch, as the word "dude," so often used, was derogatory.) Jack was a nice height, not too short, not too tall. He was handsome, with dark hair, grey-green eyes, and an obvious intelligence. He strode up to the counter, his cowboy boots intentionally scuffed to look well worn, and his Stetson hat at the rakish angle cowboys wore. He was the very picture of a real rancher. All that practice in Prescott was beginning to pay off.

Meanwhile, the Fletcher family had gone through hell with their youngest son, Pete, who had suffered the agony of mastoiditis for years, largely untreatable before antibiotics. In desperation Dr. Fletcher, his wife Clementine, and their four children left their home in Providence, R.I. and entrained for the sunshine of Arizona, praying for a cure. In Phoenix they stayed in the Adams Hotel, the best at that time, but soon grew bored with city life and went to the Chamber of Commerce to find some place more interesting.

Jack was discussing his plans with a Chamber official. He glanced away, and the family at the other end of the counter stopped him in mid-sentence. Dr. Fletcher, stern and distinguished, his little, Southern belle wife, Clementine, and the four good-looking, young adult children were asking about guest ranches. The youngest daughter, Sophie, dazzled him. She was lithe and blithe, with her bobbed dark hair and her mischievous eyes. The whole little package looked like it might take flight and dance on air. Jack strode over, doffed his Stetson, and introduced himself, saying he had just the place for them. He described the ranch as bounded on the east by the Hassayampa River, and they thought of course there would be swimming, perhaps even boating, along with all the other attractions Jack described. He didn't tell them the river was usually dry as a bone. They signed on. As he walked away, he whispered to his new Chamber of Commerce friend, "I'm going to marry that girl!"

Sophie was enchanted. A Westerner, with a ranch, and they were going to it! They planned to take the train to Wickenburg in just a few days. Jack would meet them at the station and drive them down the long, dirt road, past cacti, cattle, rattlesnakes and coyotes, to Remuda Ranch.

Nothing was ready. Jack charged through downtown Phoenix, establishing credit, buying bedding, pots and pans, everything the kitchen and dining room needed to make the place habitable. He went to the famous N. Porter Saddle Company to buy tack for the three horses that came with the lease. Whirling around like one of those dust devils that swirl through the desert, he loaded and lashed everything down, and headed for home.

THE FROG STRANGLER

Thunderheads began building, towering up, brilliant white and gunmetal grey against the blue sky. Jack battened down the hatches, as they used to say in his New England sailing days, and headed up the winding, dirt highway. A real "frog strangler" set in, and he hunkered down, peering through sheets of rain. The road, slickly muddy now, crossed washes, always dry except during storms. Some were precipitous and all were dangerous when the flash floods that came with the thunder-rumblers roared down, sweeping brush, rocks, rattlesnakes and sometimes a cow in their muddy onslaughts. Arizonans knew it could happen any time, so they carried shovels, tow ropes, food, water, lanterns and plenty of "snake-bite medicine" of whatever variety they could brew, buy or beg. In spite of the danger, storms were relished as the desert was so perpetually thirsty; rain was a cause for celebration.

What if he was stuck and the Fletchers arrived on the train

and nothing was ready? He stepped on the gas and hoped for good luck. Up ahead, through the racing windshield wipers, he could barely make out a row of parked cars. He pulled in beside them. As the rain slacked off, people began stepping out of their rigs, congregating on the wash bank. Muddy, dirt-red water rumbled and roared below, with rocks sounding like freight trains as the current pounded them along. Jack stood transfixed. The raw power hit him in the gut, triggered something deep and ancient, and he knew he was a part of it. He breathed in the muddy smell, mixed with the delicious pungency of wet creosote bush and soaked desert, sending up their gratitude. Someone yelled, "Break out the snake bite medicine!" Had a rattler struck someone? No, it was prophylactic, and Jack cheerfully joined the crowd as they sloshed down the "preventive" booze.

The party escalated from "That sure as hell was some storm!" to hopes for good grass and cattle prices or big lamb crops, and on to tales of past "frog stranglers." Like the time the Wagner dam broke above Wickenburg, washing houses, people, cows, horses and everything else down the river, Arizona's biggest disaster. Then on to stories you couldn't believe and jokes you would never tell your mother.

The flood slowed down enough so they could dig the road out and drive across carefully. They stamped around in the mud checking for quicksand. Sometimes it could swallow whole trucks. Little by little a way was forged and drivers braved the precipitous slide down, the dash across the slackening stream, and the climb up the far bank. Jack followed, proud that he made it.

The sun set bright among black clouds, and a rainbow arched. Orange, red, purple and gold streaked the sky. Jack stopped, awed. Boston was never like this. He laughed. Neither was he! He was an Arizona rancher in a soggy cowboy hat and muddy boots with a dirty car full of a future that promised to be wonderful. On he went to the ranch in time to make it hospitable enough to host the Fletchers.

With the lease came a small herd of cattle, a burro, some goats, chickens and three horses. One of the neighbors, checking out the horses, drawled, "Is that there yer re-mew-da?" "You bet," Jack answered. Old lady O'Brien snickered and said, "Yer doods are goin' to be plenty impressed with a three-horse ree-mew-da." Jack laughed and announced, "The name of this outfit, Remuda, is in honor of those three horses." None of them knew the correct pronunciation of the Spanish word and it was pronounced "ree-mew-da" until someone set them straight and it became "Re-moo-da." The Double R livestock brand was registered in 1925 to make it official.

Love Amidst the Rattlesnakes

The Fletchers arrived on the Santa Fe train, and were driven to the ranch and their quarters in the little tents beneath the mesquite trees. They had been adventurers all their lives and rustic Remuda Ranch delighted them. Neither Jack nor Sophie had ever ridden cow ponies with western saddles, but they had been good on Eastern horses and saddles, so together they learned quickly. The little remuda turned out to be sturdy and fast.

Jack had been in a military program at Phillips Exeter and was skilled with both a six-shooter and a rifle. He taught Sophie, and the two of them began gleefully murdering rattlesnakes. Turtleback Mountain rose close to the ranch, and proved to be a den of the darned things, so they spent a lot of time there, shooting and courting.

Sophie was ecstatic. There was something wild in her nature. The lovely Providence tea dances, the proper young men who helped her in and out of cars and held doors, had sent not a single flutter to her young heart. Now she was riding the range on a fast horse, packing a gun, doing in snakes, and being courted by dashing Jack. To her, he was a Westerner with a slight Boston accent. How lucky could a girl be? He was just as thrilled. Here was a girl with a background like his and a love of adventure to match his own. How fortunate for a young rancher! They quickly became true Arizonans and remained so for life.

Sophie learned to cook the snakes they shot (they taste like chicken, but are mostly bones), tanned their hides for belts and hatbands, and bleached their spines for rustic jewelry. She and Jack rounded up the few cattle the ranch owned, and rode along the fences to look for needed repairs. On warm desert nights there were strolls in the bright moonlight. A handsome young pair of New Englanders, newly in love with Arizona and exuberantly in love with each other, they were engaged. A wedding was soon to be.

On their wedding day, Arizona produced another one of its "frog-stranglers," and even the Hassayampa ran. The wash that transected the Bar FX filled with muddy water, roared past, and kept right on even after the clouds cleared. Then the bright sun burst forth promising that the ceremony would be beautiful. The tent cabins where the bride and her sister Clementine, the maid of honor, and their mother were living were across the wash from the main ranch house. The ladies had traveled all the way to Denver to Neusteters, (the Saks Fifth Avenue of the time) to buy Sophie's au courant white wedding dress, and finery for her sister and mother. Dressed elegantly, beautiful hats on their shining hair, they clambered through mud and brush in their cowboy boots, carrying their high-heels a quarter-mile to the west to the railroad trestle that bridged the roaring rapids. Skirts hiked up, they teetered, terrified, as they inched across and slid on down the muddy bank to the ranch house. Sophie presented herself to her handsome groom looking as a bride of 1926 should look, lovely and blushing under her big white hat, her athletic figure lively in her short, frothy dress. There Jack and Sophie were married, under the tall palm trees on the lawn, blessed with the fragrance of fresh, wet desert and flowers radiating gratitude for the rain.

It was an excellent California honeymoon and Sophie was immediately pregnant. When summer came and she "expanded," Jack rescued her from the Arizona heat by taking her back to California. He was hired to be the manager of The Wind and Sea Resort, on the beach in La Jolla, next to the Tennis Club. One morning Sophie went down to the shore to join everyone lamenting a beached whale. It was so sad, and so pungently dead, it made her sick. Jack sped her across Ocean

Boulevard to Scripps Memorial Hospital and there I was born exactly nine months after the wedding, on the fourth of July. In the fall, we went home to Wickenburg.

Summers in Arizona are brutal, and Jack managed escapes that were wonderful. The Wind and Sea kept him as summer manager until it burned down, sadly, after only two summers there. Even though I was tiny, I remember our cottage near the lodge, on the beach. The crashing waves, the smell of sea, and the warm, white beach delighted my small self. My mother did not work. She was there, creating a magic time. About thirty years later I found that same cottage, so I know I did not dream it. The ocean is in my soul, I am a "California girl," though I can't surf. Yet.

The summer after the fire Jack leased a small ranch near Vallecito Reservoir, south of Durango, Colorado, and our little family escaped the heat again for several summers. There I had my first horseback ride, on Snowball, up into the beautiful pine and aspen forest. Snowball was led even though he was gentle, as I was a mere peanut atop, bouncing up and down in the saddle. I was so excited! Clearly I remember how he carefully approached a little stream and hopped over it, mind-full of his small rider. I was so thrilled I let out a whoop, startling him into another hop. I held on, delighted. There are pictures of me on Snowball and another of me sitting in a field of flowers, brandishing a dandelion, a ridiculous hat on my head. In the background is the tiny log cabin that housed us. It had only one room with a dirt floor, and no plumbing, but we were happy there. Jack hung a canvas sheet across half of it for privacy. When fall came, we returned to Remuda.

Sophie and Jack Burden came by their courage and their love of things wild honestly. Both had those attributes in their DNA, from adventurous and brave ancestors, and childhoods that challenged them. They had to be strong and they learned to be creative and inventive. They passed that spirit right on down to the rest of us. The family history is loaded with travail and triumph, faced with courage and laughter through it all. How has that happened? It is in that DNA, by golly. Remuda Ranch's history tells a lot.

Witches Swooped In

When Jack and Sophie returned from their honeymoon, Mother Burden, more of a "caution" than ever, quickly stashed Sophie into a servant role, ordering her about, allowing no possibility that she would qualify as first lady and hostess of the ranch. Sophie had been raised in a distinguished home in Providence, where their black cook, "Woochie," did all the kitchen and dining room work. Sophie had no idea how to fulfill her new role that involved serving food and drink. Her first afternoon home, Mother Burden instructed her to bring ice water to the veranda. Sophie went to the kitchen, put ice in a pan and melted it on the stove to hoots of derision. In anguished self-defense she asked, "How would I know? I've never been in a kitchen!" Her mother said, "You know, Sophie was never the bright one in the family," but Jack knew better. He knew he and his bright, lively bride would create a wonderful guest ranch.

Meanwhile, old lady O'Brien, (a weather-beaten witch if ever there was one) figured if Bob, Jack and Sophie could make a go of it, so could she. One night, they came home from a trip to Phoenix to find the gate locked and all their personal belongings stacked in front of it. Jack broke in, loaded everything that wasn't nailed down and hauled it out.

Bob decided their new enterprise couldn't support all of them now that Jack was married. It was the end of the trail for the partnership, so Jack bought him out. Bob moved northwest of town and acquired some fine, old adobe buildings that he made into the Monte Vista Ranch which prospered until health forced him to retire many years later.

Where to Now?

A new location had to be found for Remuda Ranch, perhaps somewhere beyond Wickenburg. Jack still had the big touring car with running boards for carrying spare gasoline and water, and with room enough for bedrolls and tents. He and his father-in-law, El Scumpso, set off to find the most hospitable and benevolent place on the Arizona desert. The Indian reservations, though fascinating and beautiful, were too remote, and the Natives were not all that friendly. The Mexican border and north through Tucson, to Phoenix, was too rugged or too boringly flat for hiking and horseback riding unless trails were carved out. They checked weather records, tested for prevailing winds and searched for interesting land, open enough to ride and hike across

48

freely. Finally they hit upon the best place in all the State. Right back in Wickenburg!

Rolling hills, cut here and there with deep canyons to be explored, the remains of ancient volcanoes and lava flows, mesquite thickets, saguaros and a wealth of desert flora beckoned them. The Hassayampa River cut through the area, mostly dry, but stretches of it flowed above ground where underlying rock forced the water up. Lush, riparian areas were created with "Sacred Rustling Trees," as the Hopis called cottonwoods, grass and willows to provide shade and food for multitudes of birds, their songs rippling through the sweet air. Deer, javalina, fox, coyote, and an occasional mountain lion slipped in and out to drink and grab some green grass or perhaps each other.

Hassayampa is said to mean The-River-That-Flows-Upside-Down, but an Apache Indian friend told me that Hassayampa really means fox scat, and the Apaches created the up-side-down story to please the tourists. I wondered if he had made up the fox scat story to "please" me. There is a saying about the river: "Anyone who drinks its water will never tell the truth again," and surely he had slurped up plenty.

Rugged mountain ranges soared skyward to the north, east and south, while to the west, the horizon tapered into vistas that drifted to eternity. And almost always sunshine or moonshine. It was truly a place that called to the souls of adventurers, but not so forbidding that city folk would be intimidated. "Perfect," thought Jack.

Top photo: The William Fletcher family, shortly after moving to Arizona. L to R: son Pete, daughter Sophie, William, wife Clementine, and daughter Clementine. Right: John Dana Burden at Phillip Exeter Academy. John, nicknamed Jack, is the author's father.

Top left: Jack Burden in the 1920s. Top right: Sophie Fletcher at the original "Remuda Ranch," the Bar FX spread rented from Mrs. O'Brien. Sophie is the author's mother. The first time Jack saw Sophie, he announced he was going to marry her. Lower left: Sophie, presumably still single when this photo was taken.

Top: Jack Burden with his new bride, Sophie Fletcher Burden, before departing on their 1926 California honeymoon. Right: Remuda Ranch women quickly learned how to toughen up. Sophie Burden and her mother, Clem Fletcher, handle a snake found on the ranch. Sophie learned how to cook snakes she and Jack shot, and tanned their hides for belts and hatbands.

Top: Dana Burden sits behind the wheel of the old Remuda Ranch touring car. His father, Jack, and El Scumpso drove around the southwest looking for a new site for the Remuda Ranch in this vehicle, later used to transport ranch guests. Left: Sophie Burden sits atop a longhorn steer.

Author Sophie Burden, Jr. was born on July 4, 1927. The Burdens weren't prepared to have a girl, and because there couldn't be TWO Sophie Burden's, Sophie Jr. was soon nicknamed Toody. Photos, L to R: El Scumpso deals with the new arrival as best he can; Grandma Burden, "the witch," holds baby Sophie; Sophie, age 1. Photos, opposite page, clockwise from top: Sophie teaching Sophie Jr. (Toody) to ride Buddy; Toody in her playpen; toddler Toody coiling a rope.

THE NEW REMUDA RANCH
IS BORN

In early 1928, Jack and El Scumpso bought 1,248 acres of land which had been homesteaded by the Verdugo, Ortega, Hoaquin and Garcia families, to the north and across the Hassayampa River from Wickenburg. Faced by the Hassayampa on the west, bordered on all sides by State and Bureau of Land Management land, it offered unlimited access to hundreds of square miles of wild, untouched desert. Included were lush, green, irrigated pasturelands on both sides of the river. Centrally located, it was convenient to Indian Reservations, Phoenix, Prescott and Tucson with their city offerings, and Mexico, not too far to the South. Vulture Mine's water rights that dated back to 1891, came with it, a valuable asset in thirsty Arizona. A great find, a fine buy, financed in part by El Scumpso. The family was on the move. The Fletchers took up temporary residence in Wickenburg. There was no place to live on the ranch property, but, undaunted, Jack cobbled together storage for all they owned. There was a small well with a little pump, providing essential water, and near it a structure that Jack shooed some snakes, squirrels and spiders out of and Sophie and me into. It was to be our home for a year or so.

The Tin Shack

Our little shack had two rooms, no plumbing, a couple of windows with wooden shutters, and a dirt floor. Shaggy, black tar paper made up the walls, held together by Ocotillo staves and baling wire. The roof was tin, peppered with holes. Jack found beds and bedding, an old dresser, and nails were pounded in a board that crossed a wall near the ceiling. There we hung our clothes. It was home while Remuda Ranch was born.

Charley Schontz, Wickenburg's only real carpenter, joined the building crew, which was composed of Jack, Sophie, El Scumpso, and sometimes Sophie's brothers, when they weren't back east in school or working for the family real estate business.

A splendid site was chosen for the main lodge. The hills that sloped upwards from the Hassayampa leveled out in several places, the best was large enough for a big building. Jack designed every last detail, creating a lodge that was unique and beautiful. He used concrete instead of the usual softer adobe and swirled by hand great swaths, making designs that were graceful and interesting. I remember the day he brought his new cement mixer home in the back of the pickup truck. He was as proud of that machine as some men would be of a new speedboat. Windows with frames painted lovely blue were installed on three sides of the dining and living rooms opening on to views of Wickenburg, the Hassayampa and Vulture Peak creating a feeling of expansive freedom. A huge, hand-hewn door with wrought-iron fixtures opened off the front porch. As you entered, the first thing you saw was a circular fireplace set in the floor, banked in a low concrete wall filled with arrowheads, hatchets and other Indian artifacts the Fletchers had been collecting for years. A pounded steel hood, raised and lowered by chains weighted with big rocks, topped it. Benches covered in Navajo rugs circled it, inviting guests to gather around the fire to warm hands and hearts in good company. Trips to Santa Fe and the Indian reservations yielded handmade furniture, beautiful fabrics for drapes and artwork. Both sides of the family were avid readers and their extensive library was displayed on shelves that graced every wall. The dining room was furnished with tables made in Santa Fe, small ones placed around the two outside walls for couples, larger ones in the middle for families or groups, and one long one down the center for singles. Jack and Sophie sat at each end, perfect hosts, making sure no one ever felt alone. When I graduated from the children's dining room as a teenager, I joined the singles table with Uncle Pete where we developed an ability to keep the laughter going. Sometimes I was the straight man, sometimes he was. What a time that was, a time to remember with gratitude.

A dining room for children opened off the big, commercial kitchen. Counselors were hired to watch over the guest children and the ranch children, so that parents would be free for adult fun. The children, equally delighted, were free of parents. Offices, a dining room for crew, and several guest rooms extended around a flower decked patio. Jack had created a splendid facility.

Sophie named the cottage that Jack built for his mother, "Mother-in-Law Mansion." Situated on a ridge, imperiously looking down on the main lodge, Mother Burden, Kate, and Kate's son Bobby moved in. I can't remember when Bobby turned up. He just appeared, red haired like his mother, and a little terror, the product of yet another family scandal, dark and mysterious. Like Sophie's lovely sister, Clementine, Kate had married some poor guy who lost his mind and her, but not before Bobby was born.

Second to be built was the patio building, horseshoe shaped, with a rock pool, home to goldfish, bubbling water and flowers gracing the center courtyard. There were ten rooms with five connecting baths, a real luxury at a time when bathrooms down the hall were usual.

Cabins followed to accommodate 65 to 70 guests. All the buildings were furnished with handmade Santa Fe furniture, Navajo rugs, native pottery and paintings.

El Scumpso thought it unseemly for us to be in our tin shack, so he built a three-room cottage for our little family, next to a mesquite thicket, which became a hideout and magic playground for us. Secret trails in the dense shade hid us from the grown ups. We lived there for a few years, but whenever the number of guests increased to seventy, our rooms were needed, so we shuffled around from place to place, sometimes sleeping in bedrolls in the ranch sheds.

With no formal training, Jack created a ranch with a distinctive style and an ambiance that was beautiful. With even less formal training, it could be said, they managed to have my brother John, eighteen months after my arrival, between the hammering, nailing and cement mixing. On January 14, 1929, John arrived, in the Wickenburg Hospital. Sophie put him in a laundry basket in the little tin shack, as our family cottage had not been built yet.

The Laundry

Mother Burden continued to ride Sophie hard. After all, this young thing had snatched Jack away from her and threatened her as "Queen of the Ranch." In retaliation, she insisted that her daughter-in-law, whom she never called by name—always "Jack's wife"—do all the personal laundry in a washtub with a scrub board, and make her own soap. Jack was too busy building the ranch to notice his mother's ill will, and perhaps he was unable to stand up to her imperious power. She was vicious. She may have been a real witch, as she used a Ouija board and did strange things like hold séances and go into trances. There are people like that. No matter, Jack was glowingly proud of Sophie's accomplishments as a ranch woman, and that was what he focused on.

Sophie made the soap on the wood-burning stove in front of our little shack. I remember the smell of lye and tallow, as she boiled and stirred it into a molasses-like consistency. Then she poured it into flat pans, left it to stiffen for a few days, and cut it into bars. Strong and pungent, it was good not only for laundry and cleaning, but as a salve for insect bites, sucking the poison and itch out more effectively than any of the remedies we have now. Who taught her to do that? She certainly didn't learn it in Providence! Joe Quesada helped with ranch work and very likely his wife showed Sophie how. What a woman Sophie was! A New England private school girl making lye soap, mixing cement, hammering nails, giving birth, and having the forbearance not to murder her mother-in-law.

When it rained on our little shack, pots and pans were hung on hooks Jack had screwed in under all the leaks in the tin roof. A fine plinking and plunking made a song as the rain came in. We celebrated it, no matter the mud. Rain brought green grass, flowers, and mud puddles. There are pictures of John and me, joyous little urchins, riding our tricycles, pulling our little red wagons through the puddles.

When summer came and heat pounded us, we slept outdoors. Each leg of our beds stood in a large can of water to keep scorpions, centipedes, ants and spiders from crawling up between the sheets. Even so, we checked them carefully before sliding in. How delicious it was to slip into their coolness, and go to sleep with stars in our eyes. The air was so clear we could sense perspective, some stars clearly closer to earth than others, with the Milky Way arching over it all.

Monsoons created towering thunderheads and flashing lightning, and we scuttled inside as the rain sliced through the desert heat. If the little washes ran, we put on our tennis shoes and bathing suits and jumped in; dodging whatever flotsam was swept downstream.

Our guardian angels were surely with us, as it is a wonder we never came to harm. It was grand, and only the beginning of a childhood, and a business, unlike anything most people could imagine.

Our little brother Dana, five years younger than John, sadly missed out on our adventures in the tin shack. He burst on board, Sophie and Jack so busy with the ranch they barely made it to the Wickenburg Hospital. There was nothing like an anesthesiologist in town, and only Mrs. Copeland to act as nurse. Her husband, old Dr. Copeland handed Sophie a towel and a can of chloroform so she could knock herself out if the pain became too much, which it must have, as she soaked the towel, slapped it over her nose, and out she went. Her mother-in-law, ever the witch, was understandably horrified, doctor's ex-wife that she was, but she didn't leave it at that. She sneered not only at the primitiveness of the event, but that her daughter-in-law, "Jack's wife was like a peasant, having all those children!" No one paid any attention to her as Dana, a jolly little fellow, completely delighted Sophie and Jack. John and I thought our little bro was the best toy yet. We hauled him around in our red wagons until he grew big enough to make us The Three Musketeers. We charged through our unique childhood together, creating mischievous fun.

HERE COME THE GUESTS

"Break out the Champagne!" went up the cry. The new Remuda Ranch was open for business. The nine horses, with their saddles and bridles, waited in the corral for their riders, and the new cowboys, Sugar Wafer, Hank and Charley were ready to ride. The kitchen's pots and pans were simmering and the big walk-in refrigerator was filled with the best food Jack and his new chef could find. Jack and Sophie, with their New England private school backgrounds knew how to create menus that would delight the most discriminating tastes.

Especially good were the dairy products. Seven Holstein and Jersey cows supplied fresh milk. The ranch's cowboys sat on little three legged milking stools, heads pressed into the cows' flanks, squeezing their udders until streams squirted out to make musical pings as they hit the buckets. Hank's aim was great and he loved to shoot ribbons of milk into our wide-open mouths. The barn cats caught on quickly and sat beside us, pink mouths opened as wide ours, relishing the treat with us. What a bunch we were, cats and kids neatly lined up, mouths agape like baby birds, while Hank squirted.

We had a cream separator with cylinders that whirled the cream from the milk as we took turns cranking with all our might. The fresh results were far more delicious than the processed dairy products of today and no one caught anything deadly. Fresh cream made delectable deserts and we made butter, too, churning it and then pressing it into nifty little patties. John, Dana, and I were recruited as soon as we were big enough to help. Even when we were quite small we cranked the separator, pitched hay, fed grain and shoveled manure. From the very beginning, Remuda was a team project.

Jack bought a bull to breed the cows, an event we watched in amazement. Our young, innocent eyes popped out as the big bull mounted a cow, both making a lot of weird noise. Finally the calves were born, sometimes pulled by one of the cowboys to help the straining, groaning cow. It was almost enough to make us throw up, but then the cow cleaned her baby off, licking it tenderly. The little calf would stagger to its feet, search for its mother's udder, and the wonder of new life washed over us.

We fed them well, fattened them to prime and then Jack and the cowboys butchered them so we always had fresh meat. Chickens supplied eggs, and we fed our pigs the food the guests left over. Savory pork and bacon graced our tables. All that wholesome food was bountiful for years, until the state put a stop to it, saying the garbage had to be cooked before we fed it to the pigs, the beef must be stamped by a government official, and the milk must be pasteurized. (Angry at the government, we became rebels.)

Jack and Sophie created a guest ranch that attracted people from all over the world. They had to be relatively rich to afford to come, and some were famous. The rule was that only first names were to be used, and no one was to be asked what their business was. The anonymity created a freedom and camaraderie that the guests loved. Many returned year after year, stayed at least a month, and some for the entire eight month season. Lifelong friendships were cultivated.

Occasionally guests were so prestigious that we had to pull back and address them more properly. Mr. Ernest L. Simpson, an Englishman who owned Simpson Ship Lines, was the ex-father-in-law of Wallis Simpson Warfield Wales, the Duchess of Windsor for whom King Edward abdicated the throne. We always addressed him as Mr. Simpson, but we called his beautiful French secretary Lea. If you are as respectable as all that, you can travel with a French secretary.

J. B. Priestly, the English author of many books and plays, was happy to be "J.B." to his peers, but the staff and children called him and his wife, Jane, Mr. and Mrs. Priestly. Jack built a little one-room studio with a wood stove out in a mesquite thicket for J.B.. Called Priestly Palace, it provided him with peace and quiet, and from there he produced three books. The five wonderful Priestly children became part of the ranch family. They joined John, Dana, and me in our wild adventures, with the tacit, though sometimes terrified, approval of their nanny. We loved "Nanny" and found her fascinating because she had spectacular red hair and her "buzzoom" dangled over her belt. J.B. was so impressed with the things we created, our stick horse ranches and rodeos, and our independence that he wrote about us in his book, *Midnight on the Desert*. After Jane died, he married Jaquetta Hawk, a famous-in-her-field historian, archeologist and author—but not before he tried to capture Sophie after she became a widow. His prestige cut no mustard with her, and she skittered away.

There were always dogs and cats with us. They gave us the affection and unconditional love, as good pets do, that we lacked from our parents. They were doing all they could to provide us with a life and environment that was wonderful, but that kept us essentially orphaned. Those little critters taught my brothers and me about love and we cared for them with all our hearts. Bunnies were given to us one Easter, and we could not stand to have them cooped up, so, with our gardener Nels' help we made a large pen for them. What a joy it was to see them bound around exuberantly free! I ache for the billions of rabbits and other animals that live caged.

My little apricot-colored cocker spaniel, Linda, had puppies at the same time our cat, T-Wen, had kittens. Two of her kitties matched Linda's apricot color, and there they were, along with the puppies, at her lunch counter. We looked in amazement. "Is that a puppy, or what is that? A cat! A matching, apricot cat." T-Wen tried to return the favor, but she was a little small for puppies. In spite of her size, she was a formidable huntress. One day she presented her family with a jackrabbit bigger than she was. She could not have killed it, and we worried about what dread disease might have done it in, so we snatched it away, compensating with treats of a better kind. She may not have been entirely right in her little kitty head, as she also brought in some orange peels. But her love was strong and undying. She followed us around "talking" to us, with little Linda beside her, their puppies and kittens bouncing along behind.

The great old touring car Jack and El Scumpso had used to explore Arizona still led the ranch fleet. Soon a Cadillac and a Ford "Woodie" station wagon, the first in Arizona, were added. Later Jack bought a rickety old flatbed truck, which hauled feed to the corrals, and trash to the dump in the hills behind the ranch. It was named Lydia Pinkham after a remedy that was hawked around for the "alleviation of female problems." (It was mostly alcohol.) We kids loved to sit on the tailgate, feet dangling over, as the truck bounced over the two-track dirt roads. Dangerous? Probably, but thoughts along those lines just did not happen. We sang at the top of our lungs, "Here we go in Lydiooooo!" Nels the gardener drove and he must have been a saint, or maybe hard-of-hearing, to endure it.

Several guests wanted to build their own homes on the ranch, so Jack devised a system by which they could build them and live there as long as they wished, with the eventual absorption of the homes back into the ranch proper. It worked well, and over time the ranch acquired, painlessly, the Monroe, Simpson, Newton, Kettering and McCrady homes.

Two small buildings were erected on a little plateau across a dry wash from the main ranch, and J.B. Priestly dedicated them as the Remuda Ranch School in a ceremony full of pride and hope. The

Priestly children, John, Dana, and I were the first students, soon joined by guest children who brought their books and assignments to keep up with their schooling during long stays. Guest children from nearby ranches began to join us, and the project thrived. Donna Keeler, our headmistress, taught the guest students so well that they reported being ahead of their classes when they returned home.

John, Dana, and I didn't fare quite as well. Donna had adopted a free thinking California curriculum, a kind of precursor to hippiedom, and eventually John and Dana were transferred to the Wickenburg schools, while I had to be tutored to catch up.

Donna didn't last either. Her husband, Miner, committed suicide, my mother said, "Because Donna would only allow sex on Tuesday." She ran off to Tucson with our assistant manager, Carl Steibolt, where they no doubt had sex on lots of days other than Tuesday. I was about twelve when my mother imparted that information. I was baffled. "The facts of life" were not discussed, and what my brothers and I gleaned from life on Remuda produced skewed views. On the one hand, we were aware that a lot of sneaky stuff went on, whispered about with excitement. On the other hand, what the heck was it?

I was completely in the dark about sex. Mom finally screwed up enough courage to tell me the facts of life, sort of. Horrified, I asked her, "Surely the Royals don't do that, do they?" We regarded royalty highly, a left over from New England, no doubt. Mom, at a loss, stuttered out, "They probably do it differently." So I thought perhaps they did it through their navels until I gained some clarity.

Our aunt Billie, wife of Sophie's little brother Pete, had been a test pilot's wife. Her dashing husband crashed during a test run, and Billie, newly widowed, enrolled in the University of Arizona to become a teacher. Pete was at the U majoring in archeology. Fascinated by Indians, as his father was, he had been on digs all over Arizona and New Mexico, and had become an authority. Billie and Pete were both popular members of the sorority and fraternity crowds and lively times were shared. Soon they fell in love, and were married.

Billie took Donna's place as the head mistress of our little school. She waltzed into the classroom, stood regally behind the teacher's desk and we knew she was to be our honored leader. She fixed us with her gorgeous blue eyes and, by golly, we learned our lessons. She had a natural ability to teach and inspire good behavior. Our educations improved greatly but not soon enough to catch us up.

My mother and grandmothers were too busy to guide me, but they did make some feeble attempts. Grandmother Burden decided I should play the piano, so she sat me down at the keyboard and instructed me to start a little ditty. "What?" I thought, "How do I do this?" After one lesson, she loudly decreed that I was totally tone deaf and should never pursue anything musical. Unfortunately, I believed her.

In contrast, my grandmother Clementine, now called Nano, took me on her desert hikes. She sped along, staff in hand, her little fox terrier, Foxie, at her side, exclaiming, "Look at that!" or, "Can you believe it? It is so beautiful!" as she pointed out cacti in bloom, wild flowers and rabbits bounding through the desert. She taught me to "Look at that" and to be aware of all the wonder around us. She also enjoyed my company, a rare gift at that time. Little people need to think they are nice to be with. When we weren't hiking, she was always flitting about in her twittery, delightful way, entertaining the guests. She loved Canasta because she said, "It gives me something to think about while I'm talking!"

Scumpso loved to play Scoop Rummy, and he often enlisted us children to join him after dinner. He taught us well, and not just Rummy; he dove into his wealth of wisdom and expounded on Shakespeare, Kipling, the "meaning of life" and treasures found in books. He loved port wine and served us little glasses as we played. It was then that I learned playing rummy gives one a warm, happy feeling. Beyond those blessings, we were on our own.

I searched for role models among the guests. Baby Braggiotti, divorced from a famous concert pianist and inheritor of a steel fortune, told how she had tried to become a Catholic in Italy, because she "longed for God." Her figure was impressive, and she displayed it flamboyantly in revealing dresses. She swept into a Catholic cathedral in Rome on her search and the priests kicked her indecent self out, yelling curses as she went. She was incensed! Her search segued to alcohol and romance. She was hilarious, and beautiful, and I was not the only one mesmerized. Her free spirit kept us delighted and fascinated.

One day she careened down a hill in her little jeep, crashed through a gate and demolished it, all the while exultantly yelling, "Nothing is going to keep me prisoner!"

I haven't driven through gates, except perhaps symbolically, but quite a bit of the outrageousness I so admired has trickled down to brighten our family. Her love of music became mine, too. We loved to sing that old song, "Near You," and I realized, tone deaf and inept as Grandmother Burden had labeled me, I could still sing a sexy song just fine. Baby eventually found a dashing fireman in Phoenix and left us.

Luckily, there were others, like Jean Lightfoot who thought I was bright and funny and took me on as her sidekick. We wrote silly poems, sang songs, danced, and she even made me a swirling skirt with blue flowers so I could, I think she imagined, do a Can-Can. Unfortunately for me, she met the editor of the St. Louis Post Dispatch newspaper and married him, which changed her into a most prestigious and proper matron. What a loss!

The ranch manager, Dallas Gant, had come to us as a dish-washer. Jack recognized his intelligence and trained him to be the assistant manager. In time, he married Edie, tall, blonde and elegantly dressed. She was wise and unfailingly tactful. It was said, "No one ever heard her say an unkind word." I am still trying to emulate her. However, I relate too well to Alice Roosevelt Longworth, Teddy's intransigent daughter, who said, "If you don't have anything nice to say about anyone, come sit by me." People are the most interesting beings on Earth, and I cannot help relishing their dark sides as well as their good traits. And tall and slim I never was. I was short and slim, and now I am shorter and have "a generous, well lived in body" as someone wrote. Oh well.

R. Farrington Elwell, a fine western artist whose paintings hang in museums lived on the Ranch for many years. Jack provided him with room and board and a place to create art commissioned by guests. Uncle Bob, as we called him, recognized my artistic talent, took me under his wing and taught me oil painting and pen and ink drawing. I went on to major in art at the University of Arizona, and was elected to an art honorary. My gratitude for Uncle Bob was eternal. But I married and had eight children who tried to eat my paint, ending that career.

Jack and Sophie liked to keep the ranch at about sixty-five guests to insure plenty of personal attention for everyone. An egalitarian atmosphere was created, unencumbered by prestige and social recognition, so guests were able "to get down and dirty" as if they were real Westerners. There was no bar, as Jack feared people would congregate there, forming cliques and divisiveness. Instead, there was constant vying for cocktail parties in private cabins. These were usually riotous, and drinks flowed generously. Sometimes the social agenda was so full, parties were held at breakfast by the swimming pool, where guests still in their pajamas, fell in, already lit up for the day.

Hanky panky went on. Flirtation was lively, with cowboys and single (or married!) ladies delectably entangled and juicy gossip flew. Years after the ranch had been sold, old guests who had kept in touch returned to Wickenburg to visit. They pulled me aside and said in hushed tones, "We always thought your Aunt Kate (Jack's lively, red-headed sister) was practicing some high class prostitution on the ranch."

"I can hardly believe that!" I gasped. "I'll ask my Mother." When I did, she drew herself up haughtily and said, "Heavens no! She was a fun-loving girl, but she never charged!"

There were breakfast rides, picnics, camping trips, and moonlight rides. We constantly explored for new sites to provide different scenery and fresh adventures. There were a few favorites like Sophie's Flat, Box Canyon, and the Oro Grande Mine that we returned to often. Ranch crew drove out in the trucks, set up campfires and cooked great feasts of steak, fried potatoes, and fresh fruit cobblers baked in big Dutch ovens buried under hot coals. When the horseback riders arrived, tired and hungry, they were served beer or lemonade. The horses were tied to mesquite trees, their cinches loosened so they could rest. The riders flopped down under the trees, or found seats on logs while the picnic was made ready.

Sophie was famous for her Dutch oven biscuits. One day a guest who was sorely afflicted with ulcers drank all the milk she needed for them. (That was the treatment back then.) Sophie simply dumped beer into the Bisquick instead, producing delectable beer biscuits. They won first prize at the Arizona State Fair, a fine accomplishment for a girl who had never been in a kitchen until she married.

Music was always part of the picnics, guitars were played and people sang. Jack would turn his cowboy hat upside down, squash it down on his head, assume a rakish stance and sing his version of operatic arias, "Achechona, Oh Bologna, Coca Cola" and so on, his

73

ridiculous baritone echoing off the hills, mixed with gales of laughter. Hank, our head wrangler, played a mean accordion, and anyone else who could contribute to the fun was cheered on.

Box Canyon was the most favorite site. Water ran there, clear and sparkling, with occasional little pools deep enough for swimming. We rode over five miles of rough trails to a lovely shaded spot where we were met by ranch trucks. They drove up the river bed, sometimes getting stuck, but they always made it with the cold beer and food!

Our horses loved it. Hot and thirsty, they eagerly drank, and sometimes one would just lie down and roll in the cool water, the rider scrambling off, screaming bloody murder. Now and then it was scary, as a horse would step in quicksand and down he would go, right up to his belly. The rider would hop off, struggling not to sink too, and the cowboys would have to pull the horse out with their lariats.

Insurance wasn't such a worry then, people were not so litigious and lawyers not as greedy. Rides could be quite long and very fast, over rough country on top-notch horses. Accidents were almost non-existent, something of a miracle. One time a horse carried his rider too close to a canyon wall, and instead of just guiding the horse away, the guest stuck out his hand to push off and broke his wrist. A lovely lady from New York was told how to make her horse turn. "Just pull the reins in the direction you want to go," Tex the cowboy explained. She forgot the reins, and was put out because her fine steed didn't get it when she pointed right or left. Mostly, people learned to ride pretty well, and how proud they were.

There were children's rides, unencumbered by adults other than the cowboy guide, picnics, and outings to places interesting to kids. Surprise Canyon was a favorite as it had a waterway, dry except during heavy storms that coursed over a small cliff forming a swell slide we merrily slid down. We named it Surprise Canyon as discoveries and adventures were always to be found there. One great surprise happened when we were pretending to be coyotes. I made a den to hide in, in one of the caves formed in the rock canyon wall. Suddenly wasps attacked! I set up a frightful howl as I charged out of there, pursued by a nasty swarm. The kids exclaimed, "Wow, you are really good at being a howling coyote!" Then they saw the wasps and we all fled. Bitten all over, the ride home was painful, but I survived.

Three-day annual Field Days were held with games, swimming and riding events all hotly contested. Every child was sure to get a prize of some kind. Children from the six area guest ranches would come to compete.

John, Dana, and I were "hired" by our head wrangler, Hank Alrich, to feed the forty-five horses in the evening. (We were at the ranch school in the morning.) We dragged big bales of hay out to the feed grounds, scattered them, and dished out cans of grain in each horse's stall. We also shoveled a lot of manure. Before the afternoon rides, we curried and brushed them, bridled them, and saddled the ones we could, though we were too short for most. We were paid 25 cents a week, such a deal, and fancied ourselves rich. Hank provided perks, like trips to McGowan's pharmacy for chocolate malts, and Sunday matinees at the Saguaro Theater. He really was a parent to us, a kind substitute for our busy, absentee parents.

Our tennis court was red concrete, and lively matches went on. Jack built a heated swimming pool in the shape of a grand piano, fit into the hollow of a dry wash that cut a swath next to the Patio building. (There was a rumor that Liberace had designed and built it. Amazing! He wasn't even born when the pool was installed, and he never darkened the Ranch door). We spent hours playing in it. "Here's a Man" was a game we invented in which we took turns jumping in as we imagined Superman, Tarzan, a drunk, or some uppity lady would. Flips, somersaults, and quite lovely dives became our skills and we were fine swimmers. There was croquet, at which we did not cheat, like our fearsome forbear, Miss Delia. The pool and ping-pong tables were scenes of fierce competition and fun was never lacking. My brothers and I held our own with all the guests. We became pretty good at everything. (In fact, years later I shot pool in the Cowboy Bar in Jackson, Wyoming, winning money. A friend pointed out that it was unseemly for a lady to shoot pool in a bar. Darn!)

This page: The Remuda Ranch Double R livestock brand, officially registered in 1925. Opposite page, top: the Remuda Ranch main lodge building. Bottom: Ranch guests on the lawn below the patio. Jack Burden, center, holds Buck as he chats with a guest. Author "Toody" is far right on her beloved Baldy.

Opposite page, top: Ranch guests enjoy the patio at the ranch. Bottom: The interior of the main lodge featured a spacious living and dining room area.

This page, top: The author lived in this three-room bungalow as a small child, built after El Scumpso decided it was "unseemly" for the Burdens to be living in a tin shack. Left: The author's brother Dana with their mother, Sophie Burden, under Remuda's front entryway, 1948. Dana eventually managed the ranch after his father, Jack, died.

This page, top: Toody was joined by brother John on January 14, 1929. He slept in a laundry basket in the tin shack, as the bungalow had yet to be built. Bottom: John and Toody enjoy a rare Arizona snowstorm the winter of 1930.

Opposite page, clockwise from top: Good 'ol Buddy taking "Cowboy Bill" Meyers and Toody for a ride, assisted by Bill's dad, Charley. Charley worked as a Remuda Ranch cowboy. Toody sits on her mother's lap. Jack holds son John in this early Burden family photograph.

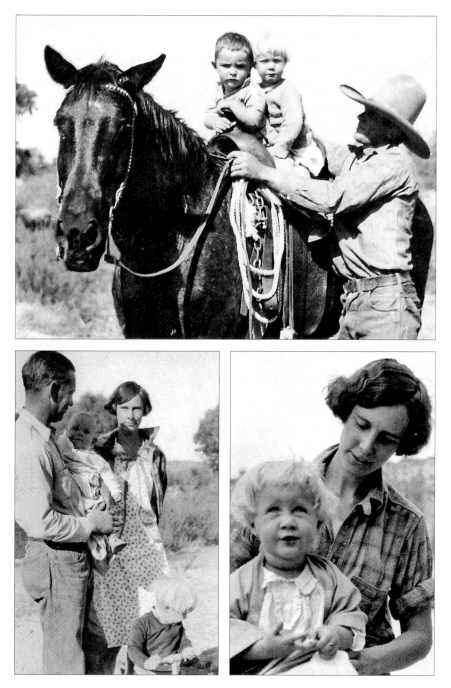

This page, top: Toody, "Cowboy Bill" Meyers, and brother John Burden play in a glorious mud puddle, circa 1931. Below: Jack, Toody, Sophie, and John Burden on a camping trip in the early 1930s. Opposite page, top: Dave Wheeler, Bill Keeler, Toody, and John duded up in the 1930s. Writes the author, "I was so embarrassed!" Dave Wheeler was a long-time ranch guest. Bill Keeler was the son of one of the Remuda Ranch School's teachers, Donna. Bottom right: Toody in overalls. Bottom left: Toody, John and Cowboy Bill play in an ore mine cart at Oro Grande Mine.

This page, top: One of many "hideouts" built by the author and brothers John and Dana on the Remuda Ranch. Right: Toody's brother, Dana Burden, age 6.

Opposite page, top: Jack Burden, far left, and his cowboys, circa 1940. L to R: Tex Adair, Sugar Wafer and Pud Adair. Bottom right: Dana Burden riding a young steer in a Remuda Ranch rodeo. Bottom left: Jack Burden, the author's father, in the mid-1930s.

Top: A Remuda Ranch rodeo horse race. Toody is dead last, pictured near the lower right corner of the photograph on her beloved horse Baldy. Writes the author: "Baldy was a wonderful horse, but not fast." Bottom: The Burden kids and ranch guests compete in a stick horse rodeo. Author J.B. Priestly was so impressed with the children's imagination that he wrote about their activities in his novel, *Midnight on the Desert*.

Top: Ranch children and guests attended the Remuda Ranch School. Left: Toody and Billy Keeler, ready to attend school on the ranch, circa 1934.

Opposite page, top: El Scumpso and Nano (William and Clementine Fletcher), the author's maternal grandparents, in the 1930s. Bottom: Toody (the author) with brothers Dana and John and dog Rover. Writes the author: "I was still in my phase of trying to be Dad's son."

This page, top: Baby Braggiotti (shown with her son "Beaver") gave Toody a feminine role model, as did the author's aunt, Billie Fletcher, pictured left. Billie married Pete Fletcher after her first husband, a test pilot, died in a crash.

89

WERE WE HEADED FOR HELL?

The environment was glamorous on one hand, pseudo-wild western on the other, and talk of religion was considered unacceptably gauche. It was worse than the discussion of sex or politics, for goodness sake. Growing up, both Sophie and Jack had been dragged off in hats, gloves, suits, and ties to proper Episcopalian churches for ritual events like weddings and funerals, but religion was viewed as something the "lowly Italians" and "Irish immigrants" practiced. One day, some outspoken, gauchely religious friends suggested that my brothers and I were headed straight for hell if we didn't go to church. Our parents snorted in derision. To us, little rebels that we were, it became a challenge and a daring adventure. We sneaked to the corral on Sunday mornings, saddled our horses, and rode to the Presbyterian Church, tied them to trees behind the building and bravely entered. Greeted warmly, in fact kind of pounced on, we were ushered in. We colored a lot of pictures of Jesus, and we heard some dreadful singing. The sermons went right over our little heathen heads. The donuts they served afterward were good, but eventually not even they prevailed, and the adventure ended. Our caring friends were in despair. There was nothing more they could do but pray. It must have worked.

The Thunderhead God

The Higher Power likes to amuse Himself by doing amazing things. If we are open enough to watch for them, there they are! My brothers and I were not convinced that we were headed for the hot place, though we had "failed" in our church adventure. There was "Something" and we knew it. We often lay on our backs on the lawn on warm Arizona nights and considered the firmament. Sometimes I had to stop because the mystery of what was beyond the farthest star, and then on beyond even that, blew my little mind. It made me dizzy and almost faint. And then I imagined God laughing and letting me know, "There is a Plan." He, or She (can't we come up with a suitable pronoun?) is with us. All is well. All is very well.

Lest you think I had some hallucinogenic event and heard voices, it wasn't like that. Just as it can be for all of us, if we are quiet and listen, we will just know. I was and I did. His existence was confirmed when He thrilled us with magnificent thunderstorms, glorious clouds and skies. Such splendor left no doubt that there is a Constant Presence, a Presence that is always present. Thanks, Presence!

Meanwhile, Back on the Ranch

Everything at Remuda was designed to be the "best ever" for

the entertainment of the guests. We learned how to create fun no matter what challenges there might be. If an upcoming party threatened to be dull, it became a costume affair. The storage shed was a treasure trove of wigs, gowns, cowboy and Indian outfits, and great and funny creations emerged. When poker games dragged, we pounded the table, Old West style. Old man Blakely used to throw down his cards and yell, "Jesus Christ and General Motors, Play!" Robert Mitchum, one of the finest actors of that time, would slosh down another drink and dive right in. He was delightful, and so was his family. Tyrone Power, another famous actor, arrived with a fascinating entourage of delectable ladies. Joel McCrea, his lovely wife, Frances Dee, important figures in the film world back then, and their children were well-loved guests for several years. There were many others; professionals, business moguls, political figures, and society folk, all accorded the same down-to-earth Western hospitality.

During the weekly square dances, if people were sitting on the sidelines, we lured them out on the floor and got them to join us in whooping it up. No one was ever left out, and the success of the ranch was based in good part on that merry acceptance and inclusion.

Back in the 30s and 40s, there was a comedian, a ventriloquist, Edgar Bergen, whose dummies were Charley McCarthy and Mortimer Snerd. Mortimer created "Snerd's Words for the Birds," including "Keep smiling no matter how happy you are!" That became our mantra, our way of life, and it worked. While it may have been forced, and even fake, as we held on, it usually became real. Joy is a choice and worth working for. Mortimer also said, "People who sit on tacks are better off." Profound.

Guests left on the Santa Fe train. We gave them send offs to remember, first with a grand BOOM from the ranch cannon as they left. Jack had found that old cannon on some journey, and when the ranch was sold, one of my sons (I'm not telling who) stole it. It sits in his front yard, saved as a family treasure. Next, after the big bang, we galloped to the train station on horseback, with pistols firing blanks in the air, whooping and hollering. At the station, stiff drinks of "Arizona Sunshine" and margaritas were passed around.

These great train send-offs were eye-openers to my brothers and me. The black porters relished the excitement and enjoyed talking to us little kids. John, about five, said to one, "You stayed out in the sun too long!" He had never seen anyone of another race, except, of course, our local Mexicans, and his total innocence was so disarming that a friendship bloomed. There was no way we could retain the prejudice of our family.

Our Southern grandmother, Clem, was furious when she found out about our defection from so-called family values. She believed until the day she died that the reason blacks had to ride in the back of the bus was that their color rubbed off. There was no getting around it; most of our family were racists and snobs. I didn't buy that, and after some angry explosions, realized I needed to be very quiet, and love our parents and grandparents anyway, even though the divide in beliefs grew steadily wider. Loving them was not hard. They were wonderful in their own ways, and who they were has much to do with who we are. Love and family transcend differences, thank God.

Rodeo

Weekly "rodeos," more like gymkhanas, were held in the ranch's big arena. The other guest ranches in the area rode their horses over to compete, ranch against ranch. On alternate weeks, we traded locations, riding our horses to their arenas. These events were times of great excitement and laughter. Lovely ladies from Grosse Point, or New York, or Beverly Hills struggled hilariously in the dust to tie goats down, three legs secured with a "piggin' string" in the goat roping contests. The men were cheered on as they galloped up and down the rodeo field with eggs in spoons, racing to see who could make it to the finish line, egg in place. Musical chairs, all on horseback, brought shouts and mock battles. There were horse races too, and we galloped madly up the rodeo grounds, yelling cowboy yells, hats flying off, leaving clouds of dust in our wake. What an escape it was for those men of importance and responsibility, and their ladies so departed from manicures, hair salons, and social whirls.

Mixed with the races and contests for the guests were serious events for the cowboys. Calf roping, team roping, bull dogging, bronc or bull riding all tested skill, strength and courage. A following of women enthralled by the sheer male power and prowess was created. The cowboys basked in the glory of it all. Some of them married those adoring girls in ceremonies on the ranch; everyone dressed in clean

Levis, western shirts, boots and Stetsons. The brides had to learn to feed livestock, saddle soap tack, coil ropes correctly and polish boots. Someone told one of those young brides to put the boots in boiling water with plenty of baking soda to take the smell out and obediently she did. Thanks to newlywed lust, the marriage didn't crash right there.

In 1930, to promote Wickenburg and the ranches, Jack put on the first three-day "Out Wickenburg Way" rodeo on the ranch grounds. Board seats for spectators were erected on the nearby slope where guests from Remuda, the nearby ranches, and town's people gathered. There was great excitement, and the event became an annual tradition, attracting people from all over Arizona. Cars lined up along the fences, and a group of young people from local livestock ranches rode over on their burros. Years later my husband told me he rode over with his brothers to watch. How amazing that we were just across the field from each other, across a cultural divide we never dreamed we would bridge.

Everett Bowman, Veryl Goodnight, some other great cowboys whose names I can't remember, and Jack started the Remuda Ranch Rodeo Association, which morphed into "The Turtles," and then into the Professional Rodeo Cowboys Association. One story I heard was that the PRCA actually began in Boston. When Boston Garden would not pay their entrance fees back in prize money, they, furious, went to Madison Square Garden in New York City. These stories fail to mention Remuda Ranch at all, which is odd, as that is truly where it all began. For years our annual Remuda Ranch rodeos continued, as weekly affairs that included events for guests.

The Hassayampa Yacht Club

The Hassayampa River that fronted Remuda was usually dry, but there were times when we would stop in our tracks and say, "Do you hear it? The river!" The roar could be heard, at first faint, steadily growing louder. We peered up the sandy riverbed, and when we could just see the glint of sun on the headwater, we dashed down to be ready for it as it flowed in front of the Ranch. Racing back and forth in front of the first wave, we dared it to catch us. Dangerous, yes, but our parents always told us, "Use your intelligence," never the archetypal parental whine, "Be careful!" We did indeed use our brains, and made it to the banks when things got really scary.

When the flow reached its fullest, roaring from bank to bank, with tall, cresting waves, we grabbed the air mattresses from the swimming pool, dragged them to our wharf, which was a tangle of cottonwood roots near the bank, and launched them into the brown froth. What great surfing, even with cow pies, and pieces of old miner's shacks, and goodness knows what else floating by! We had been told that sometimes rattlesnake nests and other creepy things came writhing down, but as exhilarated as we were, we "stayed out of touch with reality" as is family custom and the adventure was splendid. We never saw any snakes or creepy things. Guardian angels swam before us.

Did our mother worry about us? No, she did not. "Leaping

lizards!" as we used to exclaim back in the days of Little "Orphink" Annie, there she was, paddling out in the middle of the flood. She didn't bail out downstream where we had been regaining the shore, but cruised on down the river. The Wickenburg town bridge, about two miles away, was lined with people, among them the town policeman, watching the flood. As Mom hove into view the policeman leaned over the railing, waved his arms and shouted, "Get out of there! That is dangerous!" Unheeded by Mom, he shouted in desperation, "You're under arrest!" Prudent for the moment, she thought she had better not sail on by, and gained shallow water near the bank. As she stood up, he said, "My God! It's Sophie Burden!" And by God it was, though hard to tell, through all the mud she had taken on. She looked up and yelled back, "Occifer Miller, I taught you to swim in my swimming pool when you were just a tadpole, so you'd better not arrest me!" Inspired, onlookers gathered inner tubes or whatever they could, took up the challenge and surfing the Hassayampa became "The Thing To Do."

The Hassayampa Yacht Club was formed, gathering an eclectic group of "sailors" from guest ranches and townsfolk. They toasted the river when it came roaring down with plenty of booze and the riotous times went on for years. The river rarely runs like that now, clutched as the Southwest is in a long, ever worsening drought.

After those floods, backwater ponds formed in the sandy draws, and in we went. Tucked into forests of Arrow Weed, a slender, almost willow-like bush that grows thickly on sandy riverbanks, we were well hidden. We made tunnels through the Arrow Weed to our secret swimming holes. One day a splendid old Mexican, Joe Quesada, burst through on his tall, shiny black horse. We had been discovered.

Joe Quesada was a man of stature, a true Mexican vaquero, now living in Wickenburg with his considerable family. He was El Scumpso's right hand man and he often worked for Jack. They had become good friends, so of course he was concerned about us. He looked down at our muddy little selves and said in his thick, musical accent, "Hey, you keeds, you git plenty seek swimming in there with all those horse and cow turds floating around! And there might be a cascabell bibora!" (Rattlesnake.) We were too carried away having fun to stop, so we just cleared our way through the flotsam, watched out for snakes, and promised Joe we would be very careful.

Early on we had decided, growing up in snake country, not to let terror get in the way of fun. There were some close calls when we surprised rattlers, and even today if a sudden rustle of dry leaves sounds like a rattler, my heart jumps. When the distinctive buzz sounded, we knew to stand still and they would soon slither off. At seven years old we were given .22 caliber rifles, and just like our parents, we shot the boogers. We became pretty darned good, honing our skill by throwing empty beer cans into the river up in Box Canyon, where the water always ran, and firing at them as they bobbed along. Then we would wade in to retrieve them, as one of the wise things our parents taught us was to leave a place better than it was when we arrived.

Two Bugs and a Locust

It had never occurred to us that there could be any health threat from our ponds. However, we all had frequent coughs, I was skinny and seemed to have had rickets, and John came down with rheumatic fever. He was put to bed for months, and has dealt with heart problems all his life. Dana nearly died of pneumonia when he was two, requiring several surgeries and oxygen tents for months. When I was eight or nine, I developed a thunderous cough. Mom accused me of seeking attention, jealous of all the care John and Dana needed. The ranch had a nice old gardener, John Hedrick, whom we loved to follow around, and whose cough sounded much like mine. One day, my brother John asked him, "Why do you cough like that?" He answered, "I've got two bugs and a locust." In high school, I was tested positive for having had, and spontaneously recovered from, tuberculosis. Aha! Two bugs and a locust indeed. And it didn't even get me any attention. Unfortunately, it has left me short of breath. I puff a lot.

Much later, a doctor decreed me "a delicate child," but it didn't slow me down much. He said I should marry a man who could provide domestic help, that I should not have more than two children, and that I should live in low altitudes. The Higher Power had other ideas, or at least I like to credit Him, as quite the reverse happened. Here I am, kicking up dust, sliding around merrily, the mother, grandmother and great grandmother of many "above average" kids, to quote Garrison Keillor. I live in Wyoming, famous for being hard on horses and women. I choose not to listen to dour proclamations unless

I am absolutely forced to. Hope stays high, and I believe that "All will be well. All will be very well." One way or another.

There was also benefit in our parental neglect, in spite of the problems. No one ever told us not to drink out of the horse troughs, and in the Arizona heat, which depletes salt, we chipped hunks off the livestock salt blocks in the pastures and licked away, stuffing our sticky lumps back in our sticky Levi pockets. Now, we enjoy unusually strong immune systems, and can go to Mexico and rarely catch a thing.

Our Hero was Huckleberry Finn

There was a dark underside to growing up on Remuda. Our parents were so absorbed in running the business and entertaining the guests that we were often relegated to people who didn't really want to bother with us. We were the beneficiaries of benign neglect, like Huckleberry Finn. With relish we read about him, glad we too were free, but also aware that it was not always wonderful. One time my brothers and I, and our cousin Bob Pearson were sitting on a corral fence talking. We wondered what it would be like to have dinner with our parents, to have a mother who cooked, who even baked cookies! We ate in the children's dining room and rarely saw our parents. What would it be like to spend weekends with Mom and Dad like other kids? The ranch housekeeper, dear Andrea, surely a surrogate Mom, patched our Levis for us, and even bought me a dress (which I hated.) We were uncivilized little urchins.

The guest children who arrived from cities far and wide, had brand new Levis, cowboy hats and boots. They immediately pegged us as country slobs, and we saw them as wimpy city brats. Sometimes they would ask, "Do you always dress like that? Don't you have any CLOTHES?" Or they would exclaim, "MY parents would NEVER let me say THAT!" whenever we let loose with some cussing. Then I would ride my horse Baldy hell bent for leather, jumping downed Yuccas and branches. John would tell vividly how the bull bred the cows, and Dana would pick up a tarantula or a bull snake. Those poor city kids didn't have a chance. Once all that was established, they joined in our fun and times were great. But they always left, we never expected anyone not to. That feeling lingers.

The bright side was that our unsupervised freedom inspired awe. Guest children followed us around like Tom Sawyer followed Huck Finn, eyes shining in anticipation of chaos and mayhem. They could hardly believe our wild, unstructured lives.

We galloped across the desert on our horses, some of us as Indians, others as cowboys. We built great hideouts, tucked in secret mesquite or Arrow Weed thickets or hidden canyons. Once we dug a trench twenty feet long, ending in a meeting room large enough to hold ten children. Smarter than we were given credit for, we covered the whole thing with boards scrounged from storage sheds and woodpiles around the ranch and covered them with dirt. It was quite an engineering feat and remained a magical place for about a month. Then a bratty guest, a little princess sort of child, broke our oath of secrecy and told her parents who thought it was too dangerous, so they put a stop to it. We were furious. Soon after, the girl's mother gave our mom a book on parenting. Sophie brandished that book around, loudly complaining, "Why do they think I need THIS? I am a great mother!" Fixing me with her beady eyeball, she asked, "Don't you think I am a great mother?" Like die if I didn't. Well, that was the end of tunneling.

Our attention went back to the stick horses we fashioned out of Yucca stalks, each with a name like Zorro, or Lightning. We built "ranches" with wooden packing crates and other treasures hauled from the dump in our red Radio Flyer wagons. Our head gardener, Nels, taught us carpentry skills and gave us tools and nails with which we created impressive little structures. Most of our time was spent playing there when we weren't at the ranch school or with the horses, riding or working. If we managed to escape the meddlesome adults at night, we slipped off to our little ranch hideouts, built campfires, huddled around them to tell tall tales, hardly ever true, but always fun.

The Bishop's Lodge

For three summers when I was eight, nine and ten, my father managed The Bishop's Lodge, northeast of Santa Fe, and those summers were among the most wonderful of our young lives.

Remuda closed in May, when the desert temperatures climbed into the triple digits and everyone who could, fled. Our Dad had rescued us from the heat first in California, then in Colorado and next he took us to New Mexico. The Thorpe family, owners of The Bishop's Lodge, had heard about him and sought him out. When he accepted the job as manager, the Lodge was paying for its laundry service in advance and in cash; their credit had become so bad. He and the Thorpes made an agreement that at the end of three years, if he chose, he could buy the place. Our ranch horses, saddles, bridles and all were loaded into stock cars on the train headed for Santa Fe, where they were unloaded and driven to the Lodge corrals, with Hank, our head wrangler, in charge.

Jack drove Sophie, John, Dana and me in the station wagon,

one of the few times our little family spent time together. We stayed in the Fred Harvey House in Gallup, now gone. Excitement grew as we drove into Santa Fe and on to The Bishop's Lodge. We topped a ridge and there it was, sitting proudly in a valley, next to a stream that rippled over its stones, providing water music as it coursed across the grounds. Green pastures stretched in front, affording lovely views. The buildings were beautiful Santa Fe style adobe, elegantly appointed. Mrs. Thorpe, an imposing lady, and her son, Jimmy, a little older than we were, greeted us and showed us to our summer home. Rooms on the top floor, above the kitchen, with windows looking out to the Pinõn Pine forests in back and the green pastures in front delighted us. We were shown to the children's dining room for dinner, while our parents were to hold court in the beautiful main dining room. The Bishop's Lodge had a different feel than Remuda, more elegant and grand.

Clientele were mostly very wealthy Texans. Wealthy Texans are a hoot. They deck themselves out in great diamonds and furs, drive up in swell cars, and are joyously loud and funny. There were also famous guests, like Jasha Heifitz, the concert violinist. Jack and Sophie were in their element, their Eastern polish coming back into play as they hosted the guests. Mrs. Thorpe was a perfectionist and a slave driver, so they had busy, stressful times ahead of them.

It was a challenge to bring the place back to prosperity, and both Jack and Sophie worked hard all the time. For three summers we barely saw them. No one saw much of us, either. Free of supervision,

104

we mounted our little horses, Baldy, Big Enough and Mouse and took to the Piñõn and Pine forested hills. Barbara Bauer rode up one day, on her big roan horse, Bullit, and wordlessly we became the Four Musketeers, the terrors of Tesuque Canyon.

Tesuque was a valley just east of the lodge, a partly riparian stretch of land, watered by Tesuque Creek, and blanketed with small fruit and vegetable farms belonging to the descendants of Spanish and Mexican settlers. In the late 1930s, when we were there, only a few of the rich Caucasians who later encroached so heavily on the area had moved in. Barbara's family was one of the first, buying acreage higher up the creek than most of the farmers. Her father was Santa Fe's fire chief, a respected icon and guide for his neighbors and for us.

We became "terrors" because we felt sorry for the many horses and burros which were kept hobbled. Rather than being corralled, they grazed on the lush grass that grew up and down the canyon, unable to run too far away. For three summers we set them free, throwing the hobbles high into trees, never for a moment considering the inconvenience we were causing the poor farmers, which far exceeded the minimal discomfort of their livestock. We also stole peaches, apricots, and apples from their orchards, standing up on our horses to reach the high branches.

We rode to Santa Fe to visit Barbara's friends and eat waffles in the Santa Fe Waffle House. There was a quite elegant society of horse people, to whom Barbara introduced us. They had fine stables, splendid saddles, bridles, riding outfits, and beautiful horses. Hank quickly saw to it that I had English riding boots, jodhpurs, and the right jacket. He bought me an English saddle that had belonged to a Mexican cavalryman who had ridden in the Olympics. I was so proud! Our little horses barely kept up with the expensive thoroughbreds our friends had, so Hank let me ride Stew, Dan and Joe, sleek and swift, in the horse shows. Barbara and I won the jumping classes and the equitation trophies. Sometimes she was first, sometimes I was, but the competition between us was so mellow we were simply happy for each other. How good it would be if that happened more often! Joe, a bay Morgan, who won best of show several times, was my favorite, though I never abandoned my beloved Baldy. His heart was so big, and he tried so hard.

When we were not busy with horse shows or treks to the city, we created secret hide outs, spaces we chopped out of the thick underbrush where we made camps. Cozy and hidden, we loved hunkering down in them, stashing stolen cookies and goodies, pretending we were surviving God knows what. A sad stray dog joined us once, starved and hoping for some of our stash of food. She had puppies, and while she was too wild to become a pet, her puppies loved us and we nursed the little family along all summer.

There was a pond on the Lodge property, embraced by lush grass, cottonwoods and willows rustling in the breeze. Frogs sang around it. The sweet smell of water filled the air. We dragged a big log to the shore where we planned to carve it out with our handy dandy pocketknives to make a canoe. Well, it was too darn hard. Great at innovation, we turned it into an imaginary vehicle, our "Log Car," and created fantastic adventures using it as a submarine, a race car, and of course a plane. Imagination turned defeat into a splendid victory. Children who have too many toys do not develop this skill. I am grateful that we had hardly any toys, and our imaginations grew immense and delicious. To this day, we have the ability to create fun anywhere.

One night John wanted to speak to our mother, but when he got down to the elegant living room, where the "Texas Oil Queens," the famous folk and all the adults were drinking and chattering merrily away, he panicked and hid behind the coat rack. Then he was afraid to come out. About midnight, his absence was noticed, and the whole ranch was mobilized for a search. I think it was the first time I ever felt real terror. Kidnapping was mentioned, and I sat on the steps outside and prayed my little heart out. Finally John emerged, scared and sheepish. Mom and Dad were so relieved that he was found, he was celebrated instead of scolded. Mrs. Thorpe, always intimidating, descended on poor Sophie, insisting that she pay more attention to her children.

While paying more attention, she discovered that we all walked in our sleep, wandering around the grounds and into the woods, talking to our "spirits." She followed us cautiously, out into the night in pajamas, as it was believed that if sleepwalkers were awakened they would drop dead. Poor Mom! When we got back to Arizona, she took us all to Good Samaritan Hospital in Phoenix and had our tonsils out, which was supposed to cure us. I guess it did.

Three years passed, and the Thorpes were so pleased with how well the Lodge was running, credit restored, business thriving, that they reneged on their agreement to sell Jack the resort. He said later he went along with their decision, because as beautiful and fascinating as Santa Fe was, he didn't think it would be a good place to raise children. There was a lot of racial tension between the Spanish, the Mexicans, and the rest of us. The large gay population and "flaky" artists outnumbered "real" people, in his opinion, and he was alarmed when he thought of sending us to school there. He also thought we would be influenced by the glamour of famous Mabel Dodge Luhan. She managed to scandalize even free thinking Santa Fe by marrying a Native American. Jack and Sophie had met the couple and found them fascinating. Their insouciance, their courage, appealed to the young Burdens, rebels themselves, but they did not want us to grow up that wild. There were many other bizarre people, liaisons and mischief lying in wait to pollute our little minds. So we took our forty five horses and returned to Remuda.

El Scumpso

Dr. Fletcher, aka "El Scumpso" our beloved grandfather, was staggeringly brilliant. He took us on long horseback rides, he on his good steed, Blackie, we on our own little horses. For literally hours he would recite Shakespeare, or Robert Louis Stevenson, or Rudyard Kipling as we rode through the desert. I can hear him now, saying in his rollicking New England accent, "Gunga Din, you are a better man than I." Then he would punctuate his recital by spurring Blackie into a gallop, and away we would go in clouds of dust and laughter. His efforts to teach us to memorize some of his classics didn't go very far. He gave me a complete set of Shakespeare's writings when I was twelve, and my taste for good literature was born, so at least he accomplished that.

He bought land that we named Scumpso's Pasture, a beautiful stretch of riparian land by the Hassayampa, just north of Remuda. Groves of cottonwood and willow bordered the pastures, making fine forests for us to play Robin Hood in. We climbed the big trees and swung from branches like Tarzan, doing his famous yell, sort of. (It is an impossible yell.) Avid readers, we had long known and loved those heroes, and we learned more about them in the local theatre where movies came once a week. Hank, our head wrangler who essentially raised us, took us to matinees. Years later, my husband, who grew up in Wickenburg, unknown to us, told me he once sat behind a bunch of "spoiled brat dude kids," and one had blonde pigtails. That would be me. He kept trying to stick gum in them. Who was the brat? Thank goodness he failed.

The pasture had a pond, cool and clear, big enough to swim our horses in. We stripped our boots and saddles off, jumped on bareback and swooshed in, holding onto manes, avoiding thrashing hooves, yelling in delight. Our horses, Big Enough, Mouse and Baldy loved it and our dogs, Rover, Shep and Mighty Potentate did, too. Soon the pond was brown with stirred-up mud, and we were all exhausted from laughing. The horses clambered out to shake off in the sun. We lay on the grass, drying out, listening to them munching grass in concert with the frogs, birds and the "Sacred Rustling Cottonwoods."

Horses We Loved and Lost

Horses and the corrals were the center of our lives. John had Big Enough, a little bay with a white star on his forehead and one white stocking. Little John was able to get up on him by putting grain on the ground, and when Big Enough put his head down to nibble, John climbed on his neck and scrambled up. Big was fine with that, and with anything else John did with him. Dana had Mouse, mouse colored, quick and small, and I had Baldy, a bay with a white face and four white feet, and a grandly generous heart. He was a good ranch horse, but try as he did, he couldn't clear the big jumps, or display the class and style needed for horse shows, so Hank and my dad bought some horses that could.

First there was Joe, a beautiful, bay Morgan, and then Jake, a sleek thoroughbred who could sail over five -foot jumps with ease. Next came Free Play, related to Man 'O War himself, and Ligonier, a sorrel with white stockings and stripe down his handsome face. They were beautiful horses I rode with pride and delight in events across Arizona and New Mexico. Joe won best of show at the Arizona State Fair, and at the Santa Fe Horse Show. They brought us trophies in many events both English and Western style.

One delightful event was the Matched Pairs class. My friend Barbara Bauer, from Santa Fe, and I had black and white pintos, Traveler and Moki, marked exactly alike, which was very unusual. Outfits were made for us of white, divided riding skirts and black satin shirts. Black cowboy boots and Stetsons completed it all, and we were unbeatable, even famous, our pictures appearing in newspapers. We were adorable, no doubt about it. She also had a big roan named Bullit, a jumper, and the two of us were friendly rivals. No one else came close.

I had a little dream about those jumping classes. We would never come down; we would just keep on flying, like Pegasus. It didn't work that way, though. In a horse show in Phoenix, Jake balked at a hurdle so I whomped him with my spurs to urge him on. He bucked me off, right there in front of God and everyone. I was knocked out, and didn't come to for a long time. When I did, Hank was bending over me anxiously and everything looked red and hazy. I had a concussion, and was kept awake, as much as possible, sitting up in bed, throwing up my toes, all that concussion stuff, for ten days. I can't remember anything about that horse show. Cheerfully I say that I haven't been the same since, and though I say it jokingly, it may be the truth, as there are strange holes in my memory and occasional mental glitches.

It is far more glamorous to blame them on being bucked off than on just not being as bright as I wish I were.

Galloping down the dry Hassayampa River, Ligonier stumbled and off I went. Lost a front tooth on that one. Later, I was riding an excellent bay quarter horse named Jim. Galloping along a dirt road he took it into his head to start bucking. He bucked and bucked, and in spite of trying to pull him up, and hanging on for dear life, I finally realized I was not going to make it. A weird feeling, that. There was the ground, and here I came. My shoulder was broken, I could hear it crack, and my back was hurt. The other riders galloped for help, and soon I was hauled off to good old Dr. Bralliar's office. I did not cry. Julio Echeverria, a friend of John's had broken his shoulder playing football, and I had to wait for Dr. B. to take the "airplane sling" off him for me. Some tears seeped out and ran down my cheeks, it was such a long and painful wait. Julio was set free and I was strapped into the contraption where I stayed for ten weeks.

Free Play was the most difficult. While he won every class I rode him in, sometimes when we finished a course of jumps, he was so excited I could barely control him. It seemed he was going to go right on jumping everything, and there we would be, flying over the high railing, over spectators' heads. It was scary. On trail rides he pranced incessantly. I couldn't calm him. He was bursting with exuberant life. We jumped over everything in our way except cattle guards and fences, as I was afraid he would get the idea he could escape the corrals and pastures.

One day he exasperated me so with all his prancing that I gave him his head and pointed him north, where, at the time, there were no fences. "Go, you son-of-a-bleep," I said, and he ran flat-out, jumping wash banks and anything in his path, for about ten miles, almost to Congress Junction. I couldn't believe it. Looking back, I can hardly believe I rode him doing it, and it is also a wonder that no one noticed I was gone. I was only eleven years old. It had never occurred to me to tell anyone—after all, my brothers and I had spent our lives keeping secrets and riding alone.

The poor horse began to falter. I dismounted and walked him to cool him down. He was in trouble and I didn't know what to do, so, praying, I began leading him home, slowly. We walked for miles, and then I got back on and hurried just enough to make it home before dark. He revived and was prancing as usual the next day.

The next thing he did was the last straw. On a ride with guests, we stopped while the cowboy, old Sugar Wafer, opened a gate. Free Play suddenly sprang forward (I must have been half asleep) and leaped cleanly over the rump of a guest's horse that was at right angles to us. He didn't touch the lady rider, or the horse, and I held on, but it scared us all. After that I had to consent to his being sold. I cried, and couldn't even say goodbye when they loaded him in the truck to take him away. My mother swore she saw him in several movies, and I allowed myself the lovely thought that he was now in Hollywood, prancing gorgeously before the cameras. Surely it must be so. I loved him so much I used to bring him into my bedroom, where he would rest his head on my

114

shoulder. (When one's parents are totally absorbed in grand endeavors and are absent, one can have one's horses in the bedroom.)

Ligonier, Pain Unbearable

In time, my beloved horses died, as all animals do. If we love animals, we will shed tears. Their ends were of old age, mostly, but Ligonier died of what was probably a twisted intestine. His agony was so terrible, his thrashing and moaning, I could not stand it. Hank held his head in his lap, trying to soothe him. He realized I was coming to pieces, and ordered me to go home. I went straight to my mother's liquor closet, and I drank till I was numb. I was twelve years old. My brothers found me, and bless their hearts, got our Mom, and they walked with me through the night, out on the desert, in the moonlight.

Jack, Tragedy

On one of those bright days when the wind is cold but the sun shines through to warm your shoulders and the sky is brilliant Arizona blue, we were riding up the dry Hassayampa River bed on our way home to Sunday turkey, dressing, and apple pie. The horses bounced along, begging to run as they do when the day is grand and they are headed for the corral. I was riding Jake, the thoroughbred that Hank had bought off the racetrack, the very same horse that had bucked me off in the horseshow. He was almost too much for my small, twelve-year-old self, so I was riding with Hank, well behind the ranch riders. Hank was training a colt, reining him back and forth, and doing figure eights. The little bay, named Jack, was lithe and quick, each step a joy to him as he pranced through Hank's exercises. The riders ahead of us broke into a run. Hank and I were way behind, working with the colt. Jake wanted to lunge ahead, to catch up to the galloping horses. I had to loop the reins around my wrists to hold him in, and Hank was fighting Jack, as he pulled on his hackamore, eager to go. Suddenly Hank decided he had done enough training, and he yelled, "Let's go!" Jake's power as he ran sent chills of thrill through me, and I leaned into the wind. Jack leapt forward, bounding, bucking, and trying to catch up to Jake. Suddenly I heard a sickening crack, almost like a gunshot. The little bay screamed the horrifying scream animals do when they are hurt and terrified. Jake stopped in his tracks, aware that something was wrong. I turned to see Jack, his head near the ground, scrambling crazily on three legs, his left front leg flying loose and grotesquely up and down.

I felt sick and dizzy and suddenly cold. Jake was frantic, pulling to get away from there. Hank jumped off Jack, doing all he could to hold him still. I jumped off too, grabbing Jake's bit. He nearly knocked me down as he wheeled and danced frantically. My mind was cloudy, maybe I was almost faint. It seemed dream-like, and I looked again, hoping it was a dream, but it was not. Jake tossed his head, jerking my arm and slobbering white foam on me. I wanted to scream and cry, but if I did, I imagined Hank would hate me forever. I started to laugh. I didn't know what hysteria was, and I was horrified and mystified that I would do that. I picked up a handful of pebbles and put them in my mouth, chewing until they hurt, trying to stop the laughter welling up inside me.

The riders ahead had seen us and dashed on to get my dad. He sped from the ranch in the station wagon, jumped out and ran to Jack. He shot him in the head to put him out of his agony. The little horse thrashed desperately, staggered to some bushes and fell. Dad shot and shot until he was still. Hank took Jake from me and told me to go with my dad. At last I could cry. Dad said, "Let's go get some turkey, dressing, and apple pie."

SUBSTITUTE PARENTS

Our head wrangler, Hank, had been to college and was bright and handsome. He came to work for the ranch almost from its beginning, and until I went off to high school in New England, I followed him around like a puppy dog. He practically raised my brothers and me, and I adored him. He knew horses and English riding well, and trained me rigorously to be an equestrienne. He made me ride our show horses around in the arena, five times at a disciplined walk, reverse, five times at a high trot, reverse, and canter, the horse in perfect control, changing leads, head held just right. Then we would jump, sometimes five feet or higher. It was his mentoring that won us our many trophies and ribbons.

Jack and Sophie were proud enough of me to actually attend most of those events. Jack, active in the Arizona Hotel Association, always had reservations in the best hotels. The glamour, the excitement, the beauty of it all and the people who gathered there were wonderful. Eagerly, I soaked it up, learning all I could about that life so different from the ranch. Hank knew the horse people at those events, and through him I made good friends. Among the best were Al Moor, Jack Spalding and Ralph Feffer. They were my first "sort of" boyfriends.

Hank was much better to us, and for us, than the ranch counselors who were supposed to be in charge of us. We escaped them every chance we could by vanishing into the desert. But we had to eat, and when we showed up for meals, punishment was meted out to my brothers and me not only for what we had done or failed to do, but often for the bad behavior of the guest children. They were untouchable. Transgressions had to be attributed to the three of us. This was unfair and often pretty bad. Some of the caretakers themselves were questionable. Years later I was telling my husband Dom about one of them, a woman from Wickenburg. He said, "Oh, I know who she was. She was a prostitute." Yet, there was a gift in it. It became clear that to expect fairness was to set oneself up for disappointment. Expectations, so often unmet, would make life a mess of hurt feelings and pain. I learned that if something didn't come out "right," it was wisest to just think "Oh well, what the hell, Onward Through The Fog." Hank was the only one I could depend on and trust other than my brothers. Sometimes he couldn't be where he said he would be, but he always had a reason and he always talked to us about it.

Clementine

Also, surprisingly helpful was our maternal grandmother, Clementine. While she was not one to take our troubles to, she dispensed wisdom of a sort and she blessed us with courage and laughter. We knew her as Nano. Tiny and vivacious; she used to say, "Good heavens! It is really dangerous to be alive! Anything could happen to you!" There is a bumper sticker that says, "Life is so uncertain, eat dessert first." Nano would have loved that, but she didn't need it, as she was already one to eat dessert first, and wash it down with champagne. Cheers to you, Nano, for teaching us to live fully in whatever time is given to us.

However, she had another side, hard to understand and tough to take. Our mother called her "blasts" "Nanoisms." Beside her blatant racism, which included not only blacks, but Irish, Italians, Asians and Jews, (Somehow American Indians escaped her disapproval), she took instant and unreasonable dislike to some people. She hated my dear little son, Paul, God only knew why. He exuberantly lived to the fullest, and things did seem to cave in behind him. "El Destructo" was one of his nicknames. "The Terrible Tempered Mr. Bang" was another, but he was never mean, and everyone else thought he was adorable.

A lovely guest, Eleanor, often wore a bandana to protect her hair. Nano said, "She wears that thing like a Russian peasant!" One day Eleanor and Nano arrived at the front door of the main lodge at the same time. Nano's little fox terrier, blinded by a rattlesnake strike years ago, began barking. Eleanor asked sweetly, "I thought your little Foxy liked me. Why is she barking?" Nano announced, "She hates that peasant babushka you have on your head!" Eleanor, flummoxed, said, "I thought she was blind." Caught, Nano laughed and said, "Well, she is, but she KNOWS." That was Nano. She was so outrageous we just had to laugh.

I Was Such A Good Little Girl

Here is a story about unfairness and some good that came out of it. One rainy day all the guest and ranch children were gathered in the living room of the little suite where my brothers and I lived. Showing off ten-year-old agility, I walked across the room on my hands, feet pointed towards the ceiling. I ended the act in impressive splits. A thirteen-year-old boy from England made a lewd remark about my crotch. Of course I got up and decked the bastard. Wailing away, he summoned George the counselor who sent me out of my own home, into the pouring rain, alone and wronged. How awful! I went to the corral and found my horse, Baldy, and sobbing into his mane, I made a vow that I have kept. "I will not let them get me down! I will have fun anyway!" Years later, I read with delight that Oscar Wilde had said, "Living well is the best revenge." What a great way to deal with the inevitable "unpleasantnesses" that come our way. Something like fun can almost always be created, often with black humor, and if that is impossible, at least we can figure out how to endure with grace. So as I creak along into "The Golden Years," I say, "I will not let my bad back or anything else get me down! I am going to have fun, by gosh!" And I do, but it takes courage, imagination and sometimes a great effort.

Heroism

If we put our minds to it, and with a little luck, we can be childlike and wise, we can create adventures, and our lives will sparkle like fine champagne. The octogenarian whose doctor told him he must stop chasing women unless they were going downhill is a fellow who is sparkling, bless his heart. (Author unknown.) Sidney J. Harris wrote, "It seems to me that growing older imposes a duty upon us to get more like a peach inside as we get more like a prune outside, otherwise, what's the point of it all?" Indeed, indeed.

Even if some sparkle fizzes up, aging requires a quiet, strong, perseverance that amounts to heroism. Perhaps heroism is thought of only in terms of daring rescues and amazing acts of bravery, but the courage it takes to gracefully endure the hardship of diminishing physical and mental ability as we pass our times of peak performance is heroic. It can be seen as heroism not unlike that of disabled veterans who ski with no legs, or who race and play basketball from wheelchairs. Those who totter around on canes or with walkers, but who smile and keep going, are heroes too. With courage that most surely is heroic, children with disabilities, or who are ill make it unseemly for us to gripe about little aches. I think of Emily, my granddaughter who was born two months prematurely and suffers a deformation that is painful and has required surgery which diminished her physical abilities. But not much! With courage that is surely heroic, since she was a toddler she has skied, danced, and hiked— and she "keeps smiling no matter how happy she is." Children like her lead us on.

Three of my sons were born with cystic fibrosis, a genetic disease. John died when he was only 15 months old. Pete lived until he was 24. Joseph lived until he was 46, and was an inspiration. These young men were heroic all their lives. I look to them as guides for living life courageously.

I like to think of it in terms of knights on holy quests, creating lives admirably well lived. They sally forth bravely on their symbolic chargers to the fray. Cervantes' wonderful Don Quixote on his old warhorse, faithful Poncho Sanchez at his side on his burro, jousted with windmills, which he fancied were some kind of evil beings. His mission was to defend the honor of the fair maid Dulcinea, who was actually a barmaid for whom honor was just the Don's lovely illusion. He inspires me onward, laughing at our crazy lives, at our illusions and, most of all, at my self. While the Don provides useful insouciance, well I know it overlays and symbolizes something deeper. Knights and brave ladies let us sally forth into life and make it grand.

Knighthood Bites One on the Backside
While knighthood and faith will lead us onward, to be heroic is

daunting indeed and seems as likely for some of us as being an opera singer, champion boxer or an Olympic skater. Unless of course you are one of the glorious little group who can actually do those things. Sometimes heroism just sneaks up on us and bites us on the rear, as it did me. Out of pain and fear, that part of me, the part we all have that is divinely connected to our Higher Power, imposed heroism. That is the truth, even if it sounds melodramatic. It is a long story, and, naturally, begins in childhood.

Remuda Ranch had a little school where guest children could be tutored in the courses they were missing as they vacationed. John, Dana, and I spent our grammar school years there. We studied from 8 a.m. till noon, with afternoons free for riding and mischief.

When I was in eighth grade my grandfather, El Scumpso announced to me, "You are unfit to be a part of this family. I am sending you to Lincoln in Providence, the girls' school your mother attended." Growing up in the corral with horses and cowboys, I swore, spit, and wiped my nose on my sleeve, so I guess he had a point. Terror gripped my seedy little heart.

The corral was not the only influence that rendered me so unworthy. A boy named John was supposed to be the first-born, and when I arrived, Jack and Sophie were rather taken aback. They had not even considered a name for a girl, so they named me Sophie Jr. It became clear to me that I was to have been their son. I did everything I could to be like a boy, studying how men stood, what they did with their arms, their language, their clothes. But furtively I devoured movie magazines stolen from the ranch waitresses and maids. I longed for filmy dresses and so wished I could be beautiful. I had crushes on Gary Cooper, John Wayne, Robert Young, and John Garfield.

Part of being a boy was fighting, and sometimes I duked it out with obnoxious guest boys or Billy Keeler, the son of our schoolteacher, who grew up with us. My little brothers used to tell kids who picked on them, "We'll tell our sister and she'll beat you up!" And I did, until they were big enough to take care of themselves.

When I was eleven, Billy and I got in a fight at recess, in the schoolyard. He threw me down and pushed my face in the hot, dusty ground, growling, "Say Uncle!" Clearly I recall the smell of the dust, the rocks that dug into me, and a wonderful joy. Billy had whipped me. Now I had to be a girl. "Uncle! Uncle!" I squealed, and a heroic leap into a new life as a girl began.

In the Wild West, at least our part of it, women were valued for their looks, and as sex objects, or as good cooks. I did not qualify, not even, and while I was glad I wasn't a boy, it was painful to be an inferior sort of female. My idol and mentor, the handsome Hank, had guest women flocking around him all the time. One gave him a snazzy Packard Roadster. (Hmmmm—what about that?) All I could do was feed forty five horses and shovel manure. I gained attention riding my fine horses over jumps and bringing home trophies, but it was hardly enough.

Nora Hess, a gorgeous blonde actress from New York, finally captured Hank. They were married, and I would have been devastated, as Hank said he was waiting for me to grow up so he could marry me, but Nora was a gift straight from the Higher Power. She taught me to see the value of being a girl, and promised that someday I would be a lovely one. Then they left to manage a large livestock farm west of Phoenix. Hank gave me the devastating news in just a few, quick words, finishing with "Good luck." I said, "Thanks. Good luck to you, too." Stunned, I didn't know what else to say, and all I felt was nothing. Stunned numb, I suppose, was what I was.

Jack, our dear father, had been very ill those last two years of school at Remuda. Sophie had, on doctor's orders, taken him to Tucson to a "sanitarium." John, Dana, and I never knew what that was. All we knew was that George the counselor was our sole caretaker, that our dad might not live, and that we were pretty much on our own.

As a dark joke, George told us we could make big money collecting black widow spiders to sell for their poison. We did that. Jars of horror lined the bathroom shelf, the spiders leaping about, laying eggs, cannibalizing each other and stinking to high heaven. We never knew spiders stunk, but they do. Maybe George hoped we would be bitten and that would be the end of us. Well, we couldn't sell them, but they were great for terrifying the other kids on the ranch.

George was busy with the guest children and with his efforts to make enough money to finish college. It seemed to me the survival of my little brothers and I depended on my ability to win him over, to somehow beguile him. A departing guest had given my mother a beautiful, wool shirt-dress, and I put it on, hoping to gain allure. At thirteen? God help me. George took one look and said, "Good gosh, you are a diamond in the rough!" I remained in the rough. Sophie brought Jack home and we were rescued.

Jack's doctors ordered him away from the stress of the ranch. We owned a farm across the Hassayampa where hay was grown for our horses on irrigated pasture. There was a lovely, old adobe home on a ridge overlooking the green expanse, and there we settled in. John, Dana, and I were ecstatic. We were going to be a family, just like other people, with a mother who cooked and maybe even baked cookies. Ah, illusion. It gets us down the road apiece if we don't bother too much with reality.

Our poor Mom, there she was, caring for her beloved, dying Jack, worrying about the ranch across the river, and coping with her uncivilized children. And she was expected to cook? She did her best. The beer biscuits were great, and she did well with canned soup. One day she bought a chicken that smelled horrible. "No matter," she proclaimed, "I'll just wash it in vinegar. I read somewhere that works well." She did, and then she roasted it, we ate it, and by golly it had worked. We lived. She hoped that we would pitch in and help, especially me. I feel sad all these years later that the idea of cooking horrified me, and I did not rise to the occasion. But all three of us were good at washing dishes as on the ranch when dishwashers got drunk, which they often did, we had to run the big commercial machines. Since I was the tallest, I scrubbed the huge pots and kettles. I wasn't completely useless.

We were allowed to visit our dad around cocktail time, briefly, as he was not to be stressed. He listened, wanly, as we told him what we were about. I loved singing, and sang a little song for him. He said, dully, "Keep practicing." It seemed such faint encouragement I stopped singing, thinking I must not have been much good. We told him about how we rode the hay baler, helping to tie up the bales with baling twine, and how good the new mown hay smelled. We reported on irrigation programs in the hay fields and on the rattlesnakes we had shot. A dog had strayed into the pasture, and laid in a ditch, about to die, his wounds filled with screwworms. We cleaned them out, managing not to throw up, fed the poor guy and gave him a chance at life. But he died anyway. Dad tried to be interested, but he must have felt awful, and our mom was right to shoo us out.

There were small mountains of fine, pink sand tailings from Vulture Mine, transported to the farm many years ago, where it could be worked with river water to extract the gold. There wasn't much to be found, and the hills were eventually abandoned. John, Dana, and I loved to play in them, making trails, roads, hideouts and slides down the steep, soft sand banks. Sometime around 1995 the state decreed them hazardously toxic and allotted $68,000 of taxpayer money to clean them off the land. The town was up in arms over such a useless expenditure. We thought we should stand up in a town meeting and declare that we had grown up playing in the tailings, and look at us now. That should put a stop to it, but wait minute, good heavens! We looked at each other, considered our "colorful pasts," and stayed home. Can we blame our troubles on the pink hills?

LINCOLN SCHOOL IN PROVIDENCE

John O'Brien, a teacher at Wickenburg High School, was hired to tutor me the summer after eighth grade, weekday afternoons on the farm. El Scumspo had enrolled me for my freshman year in Lincoln School and the ranch school had not prepared me adequately. Mr. O'Brien inspired a huge crush, which was auspicious, as I worked my little tail off to please him, and learned more that summer than I had in eight years of school. September came, and it was time to go.

My mother provided me with a brown tweed skirt and jacket, a bathing suit and an umbrella. I traveled light. Sophie just did not care about clothes. Levis, a simple shirt and Indian moccasins or cowboy boots were fine in her mind. My grandfather was right. After all the skewed input I received growing up, I did indeed need polishing.

The Santa Fe Train was a new high in luxury, and the three-day trip was a grand adventure. A young soldier tried to make love to me, affirming George's assessment that I was a diamond, even though rough. Astonished, and shocked, amidst the excitement, I managed to escape him. I must have been a last, desperate chance as he was headed for the European war zone. How sad. We shared some delightful meals in the dining car, and some good conversations, so perhaps not all was lost for him. After all, I was only fourteen.

Aunt Billie and Uncle Pete Fletcher had left Remuda and moved back to Providence where Pete worked with his older brother William in their realty business. They met my train and took me home to the lovely Fletcher family house, two blocks from Lincoln School. I was moved into what had been my mother's room on the second floor. The furniture was splendid, old, dark and imposing, but the room was light and lovely in spite of it, with white lace curtains, white bedspread and a fine Oriental rug. Family portraits and beautiful landscape paintings hung on the walls. Aunt Billie helped me unpack my bathing suit. She had stashed my umbrella downstairs in the ornate umbrella urn. I sat on the bed and wondered at it all. Billie quickly got me to the store where Lincoln School uniforms were sold and I was ready to go.

I arrived at school dressed in the new Lincoln uniform; forest green skirt, white blouse with a demure Peter Pan collar, dark green blazer with the school emblem on the pocket, white socks and saddle shoes. The head mistress summoned me to her parlor for my introductory interview. I was scared out of my wits. Miss Cole was an imposing lady with grey hair, the distinguished kind, and a conservative tweed suit typical of New England. I could see why my mom had outfitted me in brown tweed. She smiled, greeted me, and poured me a cup of tea. I was holding it carefully, only shaking a little, when she said, "Why Sophie, I believe you are chewing gum!" Baffled as to what was expected, I asked, "Would you like some?" Miss Cole was surely a saint. She did not shame me for the dreadful transgression of gum, but took me under her wing and began teaching me how to behave like a lady. Somewhat.

The concept of ladyhood in New England, and especially in Lincoln School was astonishing to my unpolished little self. To be valued only as a sex object, or as a cook, or for physical beauty, as I had grown up to believe, was beyond and certainly far beneath the ladies at Lincoln. Thanks to Nora Alrich's kind coaching I was prepared just enough to hold my tongue. While I was holding my tongue, my eyes were bugging out, figuratively. These women valued each other and everyone else for what they thought and their ability to express it. They demanded kindness and civility. Good manners were inborn, written in granite in their DNA, and any deviation, or slip, was regarded with scorn. My mom had taught me, on the rare occasions when we ate in the main dining room, that you watched the hostess and picked up whichever utensil she did, starting from the outermost fork or spoon. After she took the first bite, the rest of us could begin. No elbows on the table, no leaning back. Only pigs asked for seconds. Do not gnaw your bones, no matter how good they look. Don't blow your nose in your napkin; in fact it would be best if you didn't have a noticeable nose. Somehow I knew, instinctively, that Anton Chekhov had it right when he said, "A good upbringing means not that you won't spill sauce on the tablecloth, but that you won't notice when someone else does." I wistfully hoped for such elegance, but it was not forthcoming. The boney finger pointed out every transgression.

Clothes? Sedate, quiet, no jewelry at Lincoln as it was a Quaker school, and Quakers are against frivolity. No makeup either. When we left the school grounds in uniform, we were to wear "pork pie" hats, kind of like men's business hats today, and gloves. Family lineage seemed important, though with Quaker egalitarian charity, several of my classmates were obviously way short on the background that was prized. Their acceptance was a bright hope to me because I feared their snobbery. That my mother and Aunt Clementine had gone to Lincoln, and that my benefactor was THE Dr. Fletcher himself, were facts I clung to like a drowning person hangs on to a log. Unpolished I was, but by God, I had connections. I recalled with relish El Scumpso's habit of stabbing his food European-style; left hand, fork upside down, into the mouth. If I slipped up, in spite of my diligent efforts, well, so what! The whole culture change was confusing. So much seemed irrelevant, silly, even stupidly vain, and yet the freedom from the sex object, good cook, good looks stereotype was grand. The emphasis and value put on intellect led me into a whole new world.

The faculty in that splendid school was composed of brilliant women, and the girls were bright. We had to be to get in. I was surprised and thrilled that I had qualified. While they asked me if we had electricity and plumbing, and if the Indians were a problem out West, they accepted me, mostly. Mrs. Giangreco, our history professor, regarded me with disgust, or maybe horror, and she let me know. Her zaps, however, whipped me into proper compliance, and as painful as it was, I had to be grateful. Miss Wing, head of our English class, put her hand to her forehead in despair as I contributed to discussions in my Arizona accent with my unconventional point of view. She put me in the back of the room with the girls whose ancestry was less than swell. For all of that, the instructors gave me the gift of the love of learning. Curiosity was encouraged, and the courses, the books, and the special events were exciting. I won the school Science Prize and lettered in modern dance and tennis, accomplishments of which to be proud.

Wendell Phillips, whom I met at one of the tea dances held with our brother school, Moses Brown, taught me to ice skate. He had placed third in a national figure skating competition, and I was all a-twitter. He didn't see me (or so I imagined) as a sex object. Probably, in that hide-bound, proper New England environment, he wouldn't dare. I thought he saw me as a potentially fine skater, which was an affirmation to be celebrated. Under his tutelage I learned to jump, spin, and skate backwards with my leg up. How proud I was! There was another boy, Billy Lindblad, who dressed in a cowboy outfit to please me. Good grief! The pith of this tale is that I learned to honor my femininity. Those wonderful ladies who guided me became dear friends.

THE EDGE OF MADNESS

My father died during my sophomore year at Lincoln. His poor heart so damaged by rheumatic fever finally just gave out. He was only thirty-nine. The tradition of my family, and the school, was to keep a stiff upper lip no matter what. "Thoroughbreds don't cry" was always and forever the mantra. Uncle Pete and Aunt Billie called me away from school at lunch break and said, simply, "Your dad has died." I insisted that sometimes people fall into comas and are not really dead. Pete and Billie just shook their heads sadly. I did not know what to do. I walked the two blocks back school and to study hall. *Green Mansions* was the book I had been immersed in, so I just sat there trying to read. Miss Cole came and put a hand on my shoulder. My tears began splashing on the page. She squeezed my shoulder gently and left, avoiding a breakdown that would have devastated me with embarrassment. Yes, she was a saint.

I was in a stall in the bathroom when some of my classmates

started talking about me. They said, "What an impression Sophie makes!" I didn't know if that was good or bad, but it seemed necessarily honorable to say, "Ladies, I'm in here!" Then I burst out and began to sob. Horrified, they put their arms around me and asked what in the world was wrong. I choked out that my dad had died. Those wonderful girls enveloped me in love and support. School was almost over for the day, so they took me skating. Some had cars and drove most of the sophomore class out to a big lake where we skated and skated. I cried inconsolably as I sailed along, sometimes backwards with my leg up.

Unable to express, or even acknowledge grief, I nearly lost my mind. My evil Grandmother Burden wrote me a letter saying it was my fault her beloved son had died, though how she figured that is a mystery. Uncle Pete and Aunt Billie were horrified, but I thought it was just another piece of excrement from an excremental person, and gave it little attention.

In desperation Aunt Billie had moved me from my mother's beautiful room up to the attic. All her efforts to civilize me had failed. I made ghastly messes. She said, "I cannot stand to see that room so terribly untidy and until you get it through your barbaric little head that clothes go in the closet and dresser, and not on the floor and chairs, you are exiled to the third floor where no one can see how awful you are." I was almost as desperate as she was, and deeply shamed, but I couldn't seem to get organized. Homework and studies were so daunting and I worked so hard I always came home too exhausted to focus on getting civilized.

Now I feared that up in Heaven, Dad knew my every thought, and I spun dizzily towards the edge, struggling to think only things that would please him. He must have been worried enough about me to do whatever dead people have to do to visit those they left behind. One night, when I was alone in my little attic room, he came. I was terrified! I could not grasp that he was showing me a magnificent reality that transcended what I knew on Earth. My heart raced, I gasped, about to hyperventilate. Dad kept repeating, "You are alright! Everything is incredibly wonderful where I am! You are going to be fine, and your life will be wonderful! I am leaving you before you faint or have a heart attack!" And so he did, and I didn't. As I calmed down, an amazing peace washed through me and has stayed with me concerning death. What a gift! He removed the fear of death, and as he said, everything IS wonderful, even the rapids in the wild river of life, though at that time it was hard to grasp.

Dad had died just after Christmas, in 1943. My mother did not let me come home for the holidays to say "Good-bye" to him. She said, "I have enough on my hands. I can't cope with you, too." Later she said she had no idea he was going to die. Poor Mom. What a sad place to be. Of course she knew, and then she had to face her cruelty to me. She added to it by saying the same thing about his funeral. She couldn't cope with me on top of everything else as though I were some kind of pariah. Maybe I was, but I don't think so. Perhaps she was protecting me from the evil Grandmother Burden. She evicted that dreadful woman, with Kate and Bobbie, from the ranch. They lived in Wickenburg for the rest of their lives. Mom, John, Dana, and I took over Mother-in-law Mansion.

My sophomore year went on five months more. My friends, especially my closest ones, cousin Emily and Nancy Gillespie, provided laughter, support, and fun. We went to one of Frank Sinatra's first concerts and fell madly in love. He was just starting out, a skinny Italian kid, but even then he had "IT." The Boston Pops lured us to my Dad's hometown where we fell in love all over again with the joyous music they played. "Carmen" was my introduction to opera, and Nancy, Emily and I dreamed of tragic Don Jose for the rest of the year. We were always falling in love with something or someone. Next came the glamorous Egyptians, whom we met at the Metropolitan Museum of Art. Uncle Pete and Aunt Billie took us to the Narragansett Race Track, and there we were, wishing we could be jockeys. We had such good times that my depression and grief didn't have a chance to sink me. School went well and I finished the year with good grades and good feelings. I am forever grateful for those two years. I got polished! (Somewhat.)

Home again, my mom's sad situation, her loss of Jack, the stress of the ranch, hit me. I asked her, "Mom, HOW can you STAND it?" She said, "I don't know how *not* to stand it." Somehow she found an escape.

SUPAI

Mom discovered Havasupai Canyon, a tributary to the Colorado River, deep in the Grand Canyon, home to the Supai Indian tribe, the summer after Dad's death in 1943. Used to hardship and adventure, Sophie Fletcher Burden was brave and tough, and with much daring, off we went with little idea of what we were doing. We started at El Tovar, on the South Rim of the Grand Canyon, in the back of Reed Watahomagi's ancient pickup, our bedrolls and camping gear piled high. It was sixty miles to the trailhead, over a rough two-track dirt road, and it seemed to take forever. Dana, still pretty little, bounced along in the back of the truck with John and me, obviously getting desperate. He kept asking plaintively, "How much further?" About the fifth time Reed heard it; he turned and said in his cracked English, "We are gitting a leetle nearer." Finally we got to the Topacoba trailhead, the only access then, before the much better Peach Springs trail was built.

Several Supais greeted us with horses, which we loaded with

our gear and mounted. It was kind of horrifying, as they were skinny, with only two or three horse shoes each, so as we trudged down the trail, spectacularly beautiful, but rough and seventeen miles long; we got off and led the poor old critters.

Evening was falling when we finally reached the village. The Havasupai River springs out of the side of the red cliff, full force, just above the little town, blue green and clear. Havasupai means "Land of the Blue-Green Water," which it indeed was. Our poor horses stumbled into the stream to drink, slurping frantically. Then on we trudged to our campsite in Mexican Jack's pasture, next to Navajo Falls, under big cottonwoods. It was a paradise, embraced by soaring, red canyon walls and above them, a towering tier of white wall. We pitched camp, built a fire and cooked supper. My bedroll felt like pure heaven, I was so tired. Dawn broke over the cliffs above, color and light streaming in on us, and I thought maybe it was heaven.

We found a spring, almost hidden among bright orange Monkey Flowers and lush grass, where we could fill our canteens and cooking pots. Scrap wood was plentiful beneath the trees surrounding us, and we gathered a supply for our campfire. Nearby, Navajo falls sang a lovely song as it tumbled into its pool, surely one of the most exquisitely perfect swimming holes in the world. Turquoise and clear, with falls that splashed dramatically into it making champagne-like foam, it was irresistible. The boys climbed out on rocks that jutted between the streams that fed the falls and leaped in. I was too scared to jump. There we stayed for six weeks.

Sophie found the tribe fascinating, and befriended them, a relationship that lasted the rest of her life. She organized food and clothing drives in the winter and somehow beguiled the Army Air Corps to fly the supplies to the needy Indians in helicopters.

The Supai liked to tease us. To them, we were pretty darned funny, all puny white and eager to lie around in the dirt and exhaust ourselves stumbling up their steep trails. One morning we awoke awash in irrigation water, our bedrolls almost floating, with a row of dark folk looking down on us from the bank above, laughing their heads off. "You like to sleep in water?" they taunted.

They ate all our candy. I thought I would just whip up a batch of fudge, but over the campfire it wouldn't firm up. They drank it from our tin cups, delighted, saying they really liked to drink candy.

Sophie was asked to sit on their tribal counsel, the first white woman and probably the first woman ever to be so honored. They wanted her expertise in building a profitable tourist business, and she did her best to instruct them wisely, but, surprise, they seem not to have taken much of it in. Indians do things their own way, and the tourism in Supai has grown rather raggedly, but it has grown. They obtained government funding to build a swell motel, with solar power for heat and for hot water. Deep in that narrow canyon, the sun hits only a few hours a day, so forget hot water or heat. Maybe someday a power line will be constructed, a blotch on the scenery but a blessing for all. We took Sophie down by helicopter and stayed there when she was too old to hike and camp. It was a farewell trip for her, and sufficiently awful that none of us wanted to go back. The Supais designated one overcrowded area for camping, and the one outhouse they put up stunk up the whole canyon. It is one of the most beautiful places in the world.

Our summers there, over the years, were wondrous. The Havasupai River, rich in minerals, forms travertine pools one after another as it meanders playfully down the canyon. We swam from pool to pool all day long, each a new delight. Havasu, or Bridle Veil falls as it is sometimes called, offered high adventure. There is a cave behind it that dared us to enter. We clung to vines and ledges, as we inched our way into it, struggling to breathe in the heavy spray. Then, out we dived, between the two streams of the falls, which shot us into the pool. Once John didn't quite make the space between the two streams, was caught under one and nearly drowned. We swam frantically toward the falls to save him. Suddenly he was catapulted out, laughing between gasps.

We climbed steep trails up the red cliffs, across the ledges and on to the white walls that towered above them. On we went—danger be damned! We discovered a cave on a narrow, hidden bench high above the canyon that had probably not been seen by anyone for God knows how long. Undecipherable writing scratched on the walls, and some strange artifacts caused wonder. Had some cowboy been stuck there? Had he fallen off as he starved? Maybe his skeleton was stuck in the forbidding cleft below the cave.

We scaled the cliff beside Havasu Falls. Cousin Bud, just above me, about 300 feet up, lost his footing and began to fall. Loose rocks pelted me as I dug my fingernails into any crack I could find and held my head close to the wall, expecting Bud and the rocks to slam into me and hurl us both to our deaths. He managed to grab a jutting ridge, and we climbed on down, shaking, thanking our angels and God. There was enough post-traumatic stress from that day to bring my climbing career to an end. Forever!

One day we hiked to Beaver Falls about four miles downstream from camp for a swim in the beautiful pool below it. Since it was still fairly early in the morning, we decided to go on down the canyon. Excitedly we traversed cliffs hanging onto grapevines and tree roots, and we waded waste deep for long stretches where the creek ran cliff to cliff. We couldn't stop. There is a family "disease" we call "around-the-next-bend-over-the-next-hill-itis." We have to keep going, no matter prudence, exhaustion or anything else. Mid-afternoon we heard the roar of the mighty Colorado, and realized we had made it all the way down the nine miles to the confluence of the two rivers. Dana, John, and our cousin Bud with amazing bravery, or foolhardiness, leapt from one cliff to another, about 200 feet, it seemed to me, above the churning water as it commingled with the Colorado. My brothers say it was "only" twenty to fifty feet down. Twenty or two hundred, it was a wild feat. The turquoise blue of the Havasu swirled with the rich brown of the Colorado creating a dangerous dance of changing colors, beautiful though terrifying when the thought of falling down into it entered our minds.

Mom's idea of a suitable lunch was a large can of tomatoes and some crackers. She was not very domestic. At least she remembered the can opener. We ate our little picnic, and realized we were not going to get back in daylight, and took off as fast as we dared. Mom fell in a cactus. The spines pierced her lips, nailing them to her gums. In horror we pulled them out, her upper lip ever stiff, and on we went, climbing back up the vines. Mooney Falls, hundreds of feet high, blocks the canyon, and the only way up is a vertical climb, aided by spikes in the wall. It was so dark by the time we got there we had to lay our faces against the cliff in order to spot the spikes against a star-lit sky. When we finally made camp, we all collapsed, and the next morning, we were so stiff and sore we could barely get up.

The Supais did not believe that we had made it until we described the whole trip. In amazement they said, "You are the first women, the first white people, to do that!" Since then, a trail has replaced the vines we swung on, and daring hikers make it often.

The Supais believed in ghosts, and would not leave their village after dark. Chief among the spirits was Supai Charlie who had died violently and tragically, betrayed, framed and done in by white cattlemen. The tribe, terrified and traumatized, buried him in a hidden side canyon. Maybe. The white ranchers may have just tossed him over the cliff. No one would talk about it. One night Mom saw a white "thing" descending towards her bedroll from the cliff above. Terrified, unable to move, she watched as it scanned her, hovered, and then drifted back up the cliff. In the morning Dana asked, "Hey, Mom, what was that white thing that came down on you?" She said, "You SAW it? You didn't try to save me?" Dana said, "Well, I thought it was just Supai Charlie." She also saw a UFO weaving up a side canyon. Darn, I missed all that. But it was a time to treasure forever.

NOW FOR SOMETHING
COMPLETELY DIFFERENT

With my father gone, the family decided I shouldn't go back to Lincoln, thinking maybe I would be useful on the ranch. My junior and senior years were spent at Wickenburg High. There were boys there! Some were truly nice young men, and there were good times at picnics, dances, camping trips, and on horseback rides. I had lovely crushes on a number of them (not all at the same time). There were girls, very different from those at Lincoln, with whom there was a whole new kind of fun. Levis with our shirt tails out, chasing boys, telling jokes, and giggling became our lives. We also did some good in Wickenburg. The town council approved our impressively presented proposal for the use of an empty building for "The Wolves' Den," a teen center that we made into a popular hang out which kept a lot of kids out of trouble. It was a proud accomplishment.

Lincoln was academically superior to Wickenburg High, and I was shocked when our English teacher had us study Shakespeare by counting the pronouns. Good heavens! The Bard must have been flipping in his grave. Mr. Fishleader, however, was excellent and his courses in algebra, chemistry and geometry whetted my appetite for science, until I caused a big explosion in the chemistry lab. That black powder looked like iron filings to me. Oh well, we all survived, and Mr. Fishleader gave me a passing grade.

In my senior year I became ill, undiagnosed. The doctor ordered me to turn my presidency of the student body over to our vice president, Roy Echeverria, and to spend afternoons in bed. Depression hit me hard, so debilitating that one night when our house caught on fire I lay in my bed and wondered if it was worth getting up. The smoke swirled and flames licked the ceiling beams as I lay there in despair. I finally got up to rescue my cat, my dog, and my books. Depression like that, suffered by so many, is amazing in its power and devastation. A fire engine and crew arrived in time to save the house.

I revived enough to go to graduation and, as student body president again, to preside over our graduation banquet. I invited the president of the school board to speak, saying, "He looks expectant." Obviously my brain was still at rest. People laughed, thank goodness.

With Dad's illness, and Mom absorbed in his care, the ranch had suffered greatly. There were painful problems to be dealt with. The school was essentially shut down, as public school funding became based on student attendance and families could no longer take long vacations except during holidays. Air travel became easy and popular, so our guests began traveling to Europe, the Caribbean and Hawaii. The ranch needed renovation, simple things like new mattresses, new

146

water heaters and paint, but the necessary capital was unattainable. Uncle Pete returned from Providence to help and Sophie leaned increasingly on him. As loved as he was, he was pitifully inept, and important issues fell through the cracks. Things were bad and sad.

WORLD WAR II

World War II brought many changes. Sophie faced it all, devastated and essentially alone. Her brother Pete and his lovely Billie left again to return to Providence. No one could fill the terrible emptiness of Jack's death. She was about to sink when along came Captain Harry C. Claiborne, of the Flying Tigers in China, who chose the Wickenburg area for a glider pilot training school. In the summer of 1944, Miguel Echeverria donated thousands of acres of his ranch west of Wickenburg for the flying field, and Sophie opened Remuda to house the student body, the officers and the medical corps.

The town was flooded with officers and cadets, bringing a whole new atmosphere to Wickenburg. The war imposed ration stamps for sugar, rubber, meat, gas, and butter. Meat was the hardest thing to get. On her shopping trips in town, Sophie careened along on her bicycle to save gas. Cowboys on the street called out, "Get a horse, Sophie!"

The young fliers were crowded four to a room and always sent to bed before dark. It was so terribly hot they couldn't sleep so they bribed our good old gardener, Nels, to stand guard near the pool. He would warn them of approaching officers while they swam through the night.

Classes were held in the living room, the dining room became their mess hall, and the medical department took over the office suites. Emergency ditching techniques were taught in the swimming pool, and the men were drilled on the tennis court and in the rodeo field. Our little family, crowded into Mother-In-Law Mansion, did whatever we could to aid in the war effort.

All our cowboys had been drafted and Sophie, with whatever help John, Dana, and I could give, took over the care of the cattle and horses. There was an outbreak of black leg disease and sleeping sickness, and we spent one whole summer frantically inoculating all of our livestock. The medical personnel decided that we should be inoculated for everything they were vaccinating the cadets for, and we had so many shots that Dana developed a terrible phobia. John tolerated it better, and I developed a mad crush on Jim Boyce, the head medical officer. A lot older than I was, and much wiser, he did not want a young twit like me drooling over him and kindly he told me to go away. Ouch.

Pat Patteson and Ed Ryan, two handsome cadets, stepped right in and I reveled in whatever my little, ignorant self at seventeen, could handle, which fortunately, wasn't much.

Pat was an accomplished pianist and composer. We sat together at the ranch piano and shared his beautiful, classical music including an impressive piano concerto he had composed. I had loved classical music ever since a young guest, David, had introduced me to it when we were about seven. David was asthmatic and had to stay in his room, so we spent a lot of happy time listening to his collection of marvelous records. I was grateful and Pat was thrilled that I was able to appreciate his concerto and his playing. We rode horseback, and many were the deep, philosophical talks we had. True friendship was ours. We were both too scared to embark on romance.

Even so, Pat hoped to marry me when we were older and the war had ended. His B-29 Bomber, on which he was navigator, went down over the Pacific. What might our lives have been? Peaceful and kind, steeped in beautiful music, it would have been lovely.

Then Ed Ryan became my ardent, though chaste, suitor. He had black hair and bright blue eyes which he said came from his Black Irish ancestry. Basque fishermen landed on the Emerald Isles long ago and married the Irish colleens, creating an offshoot race famous for being dark and irresistible. That he was, but he was a good man, knew that seventeen was not to be "sullied" so sullied I was not, but he did introduce me to something like passion. All too soon he was shipped to the European front as a pilot. His plane was shot down over the English Channel. Fished out of the icy water, he was rescued and sent home to Brooklyn, New York. He forgot me, luckily, and married a New Yorker, Theresa. They had six children. There were other flyers, and I spent those several years all a-twitter. Did I learn anything? I must have.

Everything Changes

Finally the War ended. Again we had gasoline, butter instead of margarine, sugar, and peace. John and Dana built an airstrip on the pasture north of the ranch, which several guests happily used when they flew to Remuda in their own planes. Three years later the Hassayampa came roaring down during a frog strangler and flooded it out, along with the polo field Hank had created near by. What can be done when the gods of nature decide to whoop it up? Go to "Plan B," which was to turn the horses out to eat the grass that came lusciously up after the infusion of rich silt and good water.

Sophie distinguished herself as Remuda's owner and operator. Arizona's governor, Paul Fannin, named her "Dean of Arizona Guest Ranch Women" with delightful fanfare and feasting. Sabin Brown, Wickenburg's mayor proclaimed November 7, in the late 1940s, as "Sophie Burden Day Out Wickenburg Way," and the Arizona Hotel and Motel Association, which Jack had helped found, named her "First Lady of Arizona Inn Keepers." All was well again, for a time.

The ranch was still in trouble. Three guests, Max Maxwell, Boff Howard and Squire McGuire offered to buy Remuda for an excellent price, but Sophie held on to it for John and Dana, hoping they would keep Jack's grand dream alive.

The three men left us to buy 22,000 acres west of Wickenburg and Rancho de los Caballeros was created, a beautiful ranch-resort that is more famous and successful now, in 2009, than ever. They made Dallas Gant, Remuda's manager, and his wife Edie, the Remuda hostess, an offer they would have been insane to refuse. Much later, they ended up owning the whole place! I could not hold it against them, even though they had deserted Sophie, but she and my brothers were deeply wounded and it took them years to rise above it.

Sophie's reliance on Pete was a sore spot that festered with John and Dana. Frustration and tensions grew to such a state that Dana told John he could not work with his brother, and one of them had to go. Wisely, John took his wife, Maureen, and their three little girls and went to Yosemite National Park to run Camp Curry Lodge.

What a beautiful place Yosemite was. John and his ladies did well there, but I was worried about them. There were numerous times when they could not leave their cabin because bears were skulking around. Lynnie, John's youngest daughter, needed some reassurance. A small poem might help, I hoped, when bears had them trapped and they couldn't go to the lodge for dinner. So I wrote;

"Excuse us, bear

When one comes to dinner,

And, quick! hide in your lair,

Where you will be wholer, though thinner."

John left Camp Curry to manage another beautiful place on the California coast, and then on to nine years running Goulding's Monument Valley Lodge and Indian Trading Post on the Arizona-Utah border. His career rates a book of its own, but not by me.

Dana staggered on. Sophie began to drink more and more. I left for college.

152

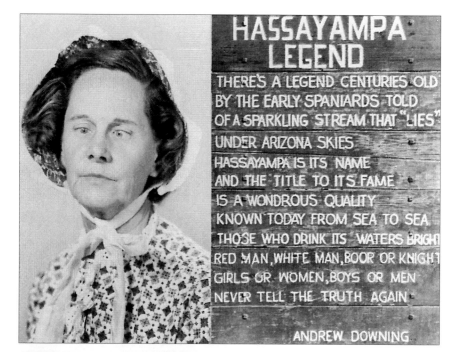

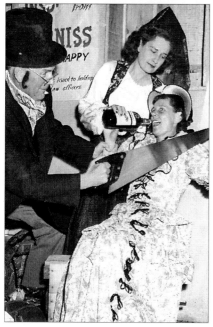

Top: Sophie Burden pictured with a tongue-in-cheek poem about the Hassayampa River. Remuda Ranch was located near its bank. Left: The hard work of the ranch was balanced with lively entertainment. Here, Sky Thurber tries to amputate Sophie Burden's arm at a Remuda Ranch costume party. Sophie receives anesthesia from her sister-in-law, Billie Fletcher.

This page, top: The author competing in bareback jumping on her beloved horse, Baldy, at the Santa Fe Horse show. She took first place honors. Right: The author's brother, John Burden, took first place honors at the same show competing in jumping on his horse Big Enough.

Opposite page, top: Barbara Bauer on Traveler and the author on Moki were unbeatable when competing in matched pair competition. The author models her matched pair outfit in the lower left photo. Lower right: Author Toody rode thoroughbred Stew in numerous horse competitions.

Opposite page, top: The author atop Free Play, a wonderful horse that only she and Hank could ride. The horse's cantankerous nature eventually led to him being sold. Free Play was related to famed derby winner Man O' War. Bottom: Las Damas, a women's riding group. L to R: Billie Fletcher, Sophie Burden, the author, Liz Thurber. The group camped and rode hundreds of miles cross-country. Writes the author: "We were real cowgirls!"

This page, top: Sophie Burden on her Supai Indian horse, Ronnie, circa 1945. When Ronnie died, it was one of the two times the author saw her mother cry. Bottom: Sophie Burden places food on a plate held by her daughter, author Toody, at an outdoor cookout.

Top and left: Hank Alrich, 1939. The author characterizes Hank as "the wonderful head wrangler at Remuda who essentially raised me and John."

Top: The author's maternal grandmother, Clem Fletcher, on Cozy. Left: El Scumpso (William Fletcher) getting ready to saddle up. William Fletcher is the author's maternal grandfather. He and his son-in-law Jack Burden bought the acreage on which Remuda Ranch was founded in the 1920s.

Top: The Burden children in 1943, the year Jack Burden died. L to R: John, Dana and author Sophie. Bottom: The author at Lincoln School, circa 1942.

Opposite page, top: The author "dreamed she was a farmer in her Maidenform bra," at an annual Gold Rush Days in Wickenburg. The float parodied a then popular advertising campaign. Bottom: The author and her mother, Sophie Burden, compete in matched pairs at the Wickenburg Horse Show, circa 1947. The author is riding Joe, her mother is on Oscar. They took third prize.

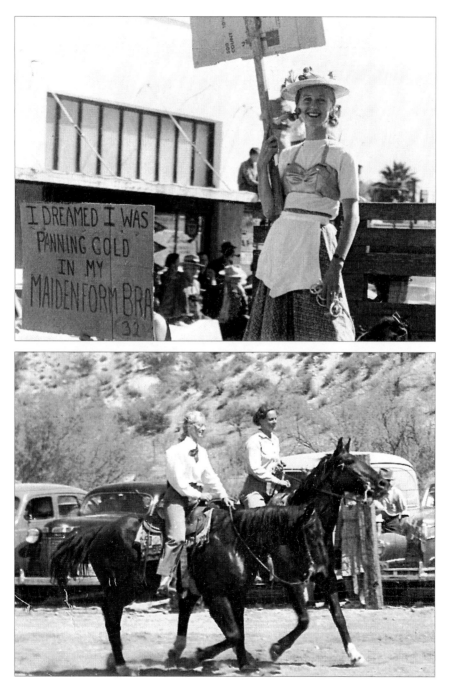

Sophie Burden's extended family. Back row, L to R: Aunt Clementine and her husband, Vance; El Scumpso and Nano; Sophie Burden; Billie and Pete Fletcher. Bottom row: John Burden; cousins Bud, Dexter with Sophie's dog Woof, and Bill; Dana Burden with his dog Mighty Potentate; and the author holding her dog, Linda. Photo circa 1946.

ENTER THE BASQUE

Dark and Dangerous,
The Basque Appears

Students of Lincoln School were expected to attend Ivy League colleges, and virtually all of them did. Even though I had not graduated from Lincoln, I was urged to go East again. Though the two years in Providence had been wonderful—the symphonies, ballets, theater, museums, trips to Boston and NYC, Maine lobster, autumn trees, the Atlantic, all of it—my roots held me in Arizona, the wild West I loved, so off I went to the University in Tucson.

The University of Arizona was famous for being "The Country Club of the West," and those of us who hoped to do well passed up some of the social delights and went to the library to study. There I was, diligently studying, when I looked up from my pile of books and "across the crowded room" sat a man so handsome I could not stop staring. He was dark; black hair, black eyes, with a dangerous, gypsy look, the kind some girls cannot resist. I would not have dared to approach him except he looked like my friend Roy, from Wickenburg.

Roy had told me he had a brother in the Navy Air Force, who was now in pre-med at the University. Taking a deep breath, I went over and stood in front of his desk like some lowly supplicant. He looked up at me, his eyes cold and piercing. I almost fled, but I managed to stammer, "Roy Echeverria is my friend, and could you possibly be the brother he told me about?" He got up and said, "Well, I am, so I guess I had better buy you a Coke," and he took me to the University Drug Store where we sat on stools at the counter, ordered our drinks and talked. He wanted nothing to do with girls, he later told me, because he was a struggling pre-med student, and women were a dangerous distraction. I must have been irresistibly distracting, but Dom kept it to himself and ignored me for months. Meanwhile, he seemed an impossible quest and I put him out of my mind, mostly.

On spring break, 1946, Chuck Williams, a classmate, invited all the University students from Wickenburg to a cookout on his family's C4 Ranch. We circled the campfire, renewing old friendships and making new ones. Our beers were merrily chugged as we laughed at the jokes we had heard down in rowdy Tucson. Coyotes were yipping in the desert near by. The moon rose, casting its magic spell. I began to notice Dom right there at my side more and more. Tingles went up and down my spine. This man was powerful! To my astonished delight he asked me to go with him and a group of friends to Prescott the next night.

Dom and I were in the front seat of his convertible, with Joyce and Bud in back, as away we sped, screeching around the dangerous

165

curves on Yarnell Hill and on to Prescott. A dance, with a live band, in the Palace Hotel on the town plaza began for me, good little girl that I was, a rather alarming romance. Dom pressed me to him as we danced, squeezing my hand, his cheek burning into mine. The heat of it made me breathless, and I asked for beer, more beer. Dizzily I sang, "Beer, beer, beer makes me feel so queer, on the farm, on the Leland Stanford Farm." Sometime after midnight we left for Wickenburg. I was embarrassed and even a little horrified at how insistent Dom was, as he pulled me close beside him, and kissed me hotly, all the while speeding like a mad man down the winding highway. What did Joyce and Bud think? Their silence was deafening.

Our dates continued and our relationship reached a point where we introduced each other to our families. The Echeverrias thought I was a dumb blonde who couldn't cook or speak Spanish. I quoted Patricia Neill who said, "I may be a dumb blonde, but I'm not that blonde." That cinched it. Not only was I dumb, I was a little "off." My family thought he was a dark foreigner and a peasant, and much worse, a Catholic. Horrors! The contention made it all the more delicious, and in defiance he courted and I relished.

He had a black, Mercury convertible, and when he drove up to my sorority house to pick me up, my smooth, famously attractive Kappa Alpha Theta sisters asked where I had found such a gorgeous guy. From the start, swept away, I ignored the red flags. I attributed his demanding, imperious behaviors and rage to Basque culture, and decided if I was going to date a Basque, I had better learn how to cope.

166

He, on the other hand, was determined to seduce the proper daughter of the Burdens. The very one whose pigtails he had tried to squish his gum into, at the Saguaro Theater matinee. The one who had been across the Remuda Ranch rodeo field when he and his brothers rode their burros over to watch the rodeos.

The Basques

Dom's father, Miguel Echeverria, came from Viscaret, which lay in a steep valley, deep in the Pyrenees Mountains of Spain. His home had been in the family for centuries. There were crests above the front entries of many Basque houses that French archeologists had been unable to decipher, they were so ancient. Their language, Euskara, was also impossible to understand, unrelated as it is to any other known tongue. Like the crests above the doors, it seemed to have been born in prehistoric times, springing independent and separate from the rest of the world. The belief is that the Basques were descended directly from Cro-Magnon Man, though Uncle Pete Fletcher, archeologist, thought it more likely they were from the Neanderthals. (He enjoyed denigrating Dom every chance he got and intended it as an insult.) They were the first people to inhabit the Iberian Peninsula, and are possibly even descended from a thirteen million-year-old ape discovered recently in Spain. "Science Magazine" proposes that this ape is the last probable ancestor to all living humans and great apes. Or they may have descended from the very large people who walked from the Moldavi Gorge, or wherever it was in Africa, all the way to Spain. The theory is

167

that they were so tall they could create the splendid art up on the ceilings and high on the walls of the Lascaux caverns in southern France. My son David, who has read extensively about his Basque heritage, snorted, "Hah! You think those Basques didn't have ladders? They did not come from Africa." Since no one really knows, we are allowed to think what we want.

From whomever they evolved, they have held their land from the beginning of history on the Iberian Peninsula against invaders from Europe, Spain and Africa, fiercely guarding their nearly impenetrable Pyrenees Mountains. Capable of guile and practical accommodation, they also managed political maneuvers that allowed invaders to stay awhile, leaving whatever largesse could be realized, but only for a while, and never to integrate. They guarded their racial purity with a pride as impenetrable as the Pyrenees. Inbreeding was the result, but strangely, rather than diminishing them, a race famous for strength and agility evolved. They have two Basque "looks." Some are tall and angular, as was Dom's father, and others are short and stocky, like his mother. Dom was somewhere between, blessed with the best of both. About 60% of Basques have RH-negative blood, which probably explains a high rate of infant mortality. This has perhaps helped to prevent overpopulation of the small country.

As well as physical strength and agility, they are, as a race, intelligent and industrious, and it is said that they may control as much as two thirds of the wealth in Northern Spain with their industries and their banking prowess. Their culture and traditions are etched in Pyrenees granite and comprise a cohesive mass of strength. Their great pride is well justified, if sometimes a little grating.

Dom's mother, Vicencia Martinez Erro, came from Espinal, not far from Viscaret. The two little towns sat in their valleys, red tile roofs above white stucco houses two or three stories high. As with the Echeverrias, the people of Espinal raised practically everything they needed.

Dom's father, Miguel, was sent into the mountains when he was seven to herd sheep, alone for weeks, as were most Basque children. The ewes, called Lachas, were milked and wonderful cheeses were made. The sheep also supplied wool that was spun and woven for their use or for sale. They ate lamb and mutton, a lot of it, and their delicious recipes have come down to us. Cattle, pigs and poultry were grazed on the emerald meadows that circled their villages supplying meat and eggs.

In winter, when icy winds howled down the high mountains and snow flew, they brought their animals into the stables on the first floors of their houses, or in to the basements, where their heat rose up to augment the wood burning cook stoves and fire places. The rich fertilizer that piled up all winter fed their gardens when spring sprang forth again. Vegetables, the few fruits and the riotous flowers that could weather the altitude and cool climate, surrounded their homes lushly.

The summer of 1969, Dom took our seven children and me to Europe and Spain to meet the relatives. We learned about the "central heating" plan and all about their fertilizer. Urdaniz was home to

169

Dom's cousins Policarpo and Juan Oroz, and their mother was our hostess. She made the children hot chocolate by dumping sugar and chocolate into flour and water, which they politely survived. Dom and I were served wine that was equally hard to get down. Little Sophie, nine years old, asked to go to the bathroom. Tia (aunt) pointed down the stairs. Soon Sophie came back up and whispered to me, "There is no bathroom down there. Only cows." I whispered to Dom, who knew the custom. "You go between the cows." So she did, as the relatives had been doing for centuries. The cows seemed to enjoy the company. Many years later cousin Policarpo worked for us in Colorado and Wyoming. He took his wages in sheep, sold them and made a lot of money. When he returned to Urdaniz, he had a splendid bathroom installed. We were really glad to hear that. But back to life in the Pyrenees.

Nearly self-sufficient, what little they couldn't produce, they bought, bartered, or smuggled in. They prospered, slipping over the border between France and Spain with forbidden guns, their much sought-after huge wheels of Lacha cheese and whatever contraband would turn a profit. Silently they slipped into the forests, up hidden trails, over the high passes on horses and donkeys as tough and strong as they were. Accepted commerce, it benefitted the whole village, so secrecy was tight and protected them from generation to generation. When the smugglers encountered French or Spanish Border Patrol, they quickly did the officers in. The impassable and obscure, deep clefts often held skeletons with bullet holes in their skulls. Dom's father remembered vividly and loved to tell how when he was seven years old, the gendarmes spotted them as they returned from a smuggling trip. They were fording a stream when the soldiers shouted orders to surrender, which they ignored. The soldiers began to shoot. Bullets splatted in the water around little Miguel, but slyly they slithered up into their secret hideouts and got away. He never mentioned being afraid.

Their traditional Basque laws, the "fueros," demanded that the eldest son inherit all of the property, because if it was divided among the many children, no one would inherit holdings sufficient to sustain anyone. The younger men emigrated or became priests or monks, and the girls were either married off, joined convents, or left the country. One daughter was always held back to care for the aging parents, what sad luck!

When Miguel Echeverria (spelled Etxeberria in Euskara, the Basque language) turned eighteen, he left for America, even though he was the eldest and could have succeeded his father, the Mayor of Viscaret, in local prominence. Or he could have stayed and prospered as a Pelota star, as he was already a famous player. (Pelota is a Basque ball game played on a three-sided, walled court. Florida has imported it as the popular game Jai Alai.) But there were many children and he dreamed of making a fortune in the land of opportunity so that he could help his family.

A rancher near Bakersville, California, hired him as a sheep-herder. As in Spain, he was left alone in the mountains with a band of sheep. The foreman who delivered supplies liked the tall, laughing young man and taught him math and to read and write in English. Was that man a guardian angel? He gave Miguel the ability to do amazing things in his life.

Miguel took his wages in sheep rather than money, bred them to increase his flock, spent nothing, and maneuvered into a financial position that enabled him, during the Depression, to start buying ranches. Initially, he had partners, other ambitious young Basques, but he was able to buy them out in time. He amassed impressive holdings, including two large properties in northern Arizona for summer range, and two equally big spreads near Wickenburg for winter grazing.

Vicencia, Dom's mother, grew up her father's slave. As soon as she could follow him, he took her up into the dark forests that surrounded Espinal to cut wood and gather mushrooms. The labor was gruelingly hard, but she endured it. Her father was a Spaniard, a Martinez, and the cause of deep shame to her, as the Basques did not marry out of their race. He was an alcoholic, and no telling what that little girl suffered. In adulthood, she barely covered her rage with spirit and sparkle, but there were things she said and did that seemed to me to have come from the deep wounds of childhood abuse. She escaped her father in her teens when the family, short of money, hired her out as a maid. Essentially they sold her as a slave and she was worked nearly to death. Her only salvation was her escapes to town celebrations, where the beautiful way she danced the Basque Jota won her fame.

When Vicencia was sixteen she struggled to escape. Her older sister, Maria, had been contracted to be a maid in a Basque hotel in Flagstaff, Arizona, and Vicencia fought to go with her. Heroines both, speaking not a word of English, they made the voyage across the Atlantic, negotiated Ellis Island, New York City, and the train ride across the vast U.S.A.. How amazed they were at it all, and how glad to be greeted by their Basque employer in Flagstaff!

Miguel spotted Vicencia at Mass and in a short time decided she was for him. "Hi, Beautiful" he said, in Euskara, and they started a love affair that lasted until "death did them part," 58 years later. They were married in Flagstaff, with a Basque feast, dancing and celebration.

Vicencia longed to dance her joyous and beautiful Jota at the gatherings of the local sheep ranchers. She bought material and made a red silk dress for the parties but when she put it on Miguel, seventeen years older, feared a younger man would snatch her, and he forbade her to wear that "slut dress." She ripped it off without a moment's pause and stuffed it in the wood-burning stove to go up in smoke along with her dreams. Miguel sat stunned, as he grasped the fact he had married a woman who was quite a "handful," and she was. Her years in the forest with her father had made her tough, strong, and resilient. She could do anything, which was fortunate.

Miguel put her on his Cross Mountain Ranch, rough and primitive, forty miles from Seligman, the nearest town, over a two-track dirt road, and left her. He had other ranches and many sheep to tend. Alone, with a burgeoning herd of children, she chopped wood for the stove, and heated water that she pumped by hand from a well for laundry done in a tub with a scrub board. Like my mother, she made her own soap. Unlike my mother, she cooked mountains of food.

When the children were hurt or sick, she cared for them with Basque remedies, and miraculously everyone survived, except little Anthony who was born in the Wickenburg Hospital and died three days later. Vicencia blamed Dr. and Mrs. Copeland for not taking proper care of the poor little fellow. He was buried in the Garcia Cemetery in Wickenburg. Most of the twelve children were born at home, except Dom who was born in Burgete, Navarra, Spain while his parents were visiting family.

Vicencia must have been a desperate mother and she took desperate measures to keep her brood manageable. Dom was stubborn about toilet training (because they didn't have one?) To break him, when he was three, she held him by his feet and shoved his little head down the outhouse hole. It worked. He remembered it with horror all his life. Always hungry, he liked to steal things to eat, and for this she beat him with kindling wood and the flat of her big knife. Once, his thumb was nearly cut off as he defended his head from the blows of that knife. His thumb was deformed and he had scars on his back and legs from his mother's beatings. I imagine him as a dark, lively little fellow, full of mischief and full of pain. His mother said he was the worst child she had ever known, and she hated him, a strange thing to tell your son's fiancée. He told me that one of the happiest days of his life was when he grew big enough to outrun her. He could not remember either his mother or his father ever displaying any affection. As a middle child, the fourth of twelve, he was lost in the stampede.

His older brothers were treated like kings, and his oldest sister,

Josephine, was the heroine child, her mother's right hand helper. The younger ones seemed to just go along with the flow. Everyone worked hard, the girls in the house, and the boys with the sheep and cattle. The family made a grand exodus from their winter home in Wickenburg as soon as school was out, to the summer ranches in northern Arizona. All the children helped load several trucks with supplies, including chickens, milk goats and horses. When they arrived at the Cross Mountain Sheep Company headquarters, they went right to work. Fences had to be mended, wood must be chopped for the cook stove, and everything had to be put in order.

When Dom was only six or seven, his father started sending him out to herd a band of sheep every summer. It seemed natural, as Miguel had been sent out all by himself to tend sheep when he was just a little fellow. Dom was a given a good sheep dog and an old Mexican cook, so he was not entirely alone. The cook taught him how to make sheep herder bread and other great Basque and Mexican dishes on their little camp stove. The two of them saw only whoever brought supplies to their camp every two or three weeks. It was during those lonely summers that Dom developed his knowledge and love of sheep. Except for his dog, they were his only companions from dawn until dark. He also learned about the plants and grasses they ate, and he grew to love all wild things. One day he counted all the different kinds of flowers on his range and told me, years later, with delight and wonder, that there were fifty-two.

Coyotes howled at night, and Dom learned to imitate them so

well they answered him and "conversations" were held. An odd "synchronicity" was that John, Dana, and I developed the same weird skill and loved to amaze the guest children by howling so well the coyotes would answer us. As far apart as we were, how much we shared.

A pack burro carried their camp to new ranges as the sheep ate down their forage and had to be moved. Dom learned from him to bray so convincingly that he boasted, "Burros think I am one of them." One of them? He let himself in for some fine jokes about that.

One day, many years later, we drove past a pasture where there were some bulls. Dom said, "Watch this," and he got out, leaned on the fence and began making angry bull noises. The bulls, confused at first, decided the snorts and growls must be coming from each other. That man leaning on the fence surely could not be the source. They began pawing up dust furiously, doing their own bellowing, challenging each other to fight. Dom stopped as he did not want them to really get into it. He also knew how to sound like a cow in heat, a plaintive, high noise that might have been a whine if it were not so loud, which further confused those poor bulls. He was not a horse or dog whisperer, but a burro brayer, a cow squealer, a bull roarer, and a coyote howler.

All of the Echeverria children excelled in school, both scholastically and in sports, even though Dom flunked first grade because he couldn't speak English. All of them became Valedictorians, and most held class offices. They were immensely popular.

World War II was thundering along when Dom graduated from Wickenburg High. He enlisted in the Navy, was sent to boot camp

176

in San Diego and then to the Navy dental corps. His intelligence and proficiency so impressed the dentists that they let him fill teeth and they urged him to study dentistry when the War was over. A billboard announced tests for officer training school, so he signed up. In the entire country he placed fourth highest and was immediately sent to the Navy Air Corps. Studies began in San Louis Obispo, California, and continued at the University of Iowa. Flight School was just beginning when the War ended, and Dom struggled with the decision to become a pilot, stay in the Navy, or leave with the GI Bill to study dentistry. Dentistry won, but Dr. Bralliar, who had cared for all of us most of our lives, convinced Dom that he should be a medical doctor. He began premedical study at the University of Arizona.

Miguel and Vicencia thought college was a frivolous waste of time and money, and though a few of their eleven children made starts, most aborted quickly. Josephine was to begin study at Arizona State University. Her assigned roommate was a Mexican, and Miguel was so incensed that his daughter would be so denigrated that he snatched her out of college. All that was left for her to do was marry.

Robert broke his leg the first day of football practice and limped home. Rudy came to Colorado to live with us and go to college there, but he wasn't tall enough to get on the varsity basketball team and left in disgust. Only Yvonne, Glady, Roy and Dom, all brilliant, graduated. Miguel and Vicencia thought perhaps being a doctor wasn't so bad, so Dom was not opposed. At first.

When Dom entered the University of Colorado, as a pre-med

student, right after we were married, his mother gave me holy hell for "making him go off to that hot bed of communism," as if I had anything to do with it. She was not happy with me and zapped me every chance she got. My infamous tendency to say the wrong thing no doubt contributed.

Dom brought me to a Thanksgiving dinner at the family home when we were engaged. The living and dining rooms were filled with tables pulled together, covered elegantly with Vicencia's hand embroidered, Spanish tablecloths and set with their best china and silver. It was to be a grand feast. I was seated next to Dom's brother Julio, who was a close friend of my brother John's. As the feast progressed and delicious Basque dishes were passed around, Julio stacked his plate high. He gnawed the bones of chickens and lamb chops and then he stacked them on the beautiful, white linen tablecloth in front of his plate. As I observed, more deviations from strict Lincoln School and Remuda Ranch manners went on. I was delighted! It was all so easy, so loud, and so friendly! After dinner Vicencia asked me, "How did you like it?" I said, enthusiastically, "It was wonderful! I felt so at home and I didn't have to struggle with my good manners!" She never forgave me. It was very wise of Dom to move us out of Arizona.

The Echeverrias were a remarkable family. Every three years they would stage a family reunion to which most came, even ten or twenty all the way from Spain and France. (There is one branch of the clan that is French Basque, a division from Spanish that is political, as France and Spain drew their boundary right through the seven Basque provinces, three on the French side, four in Spain. Rivalry began. Not surprisingly, the French think they are far better than the Spanish.) Basques are great at celebrating and the reunions were riotous fun. Stories were exchanged, delectable Basque food loaded down long tables and Botas, the leather bags Basques carry wine in, were passed merrily around, wine squirted in long steams into mouths. Chess, the Basque card game moose, basketball and other sports went on noisily. There are group pictures of these times that cause wonder. More than three hundred good-looking people, from grey haired to newborn, have sprung from those three old "Bascos," Fermin, Matias and Miguel and their wives who emigrated from Spain in the Twenties.

Vicencia and Miguel produced twelve children, one of whom died in infancy, but the rest produced fifty-three grandchildren. I have lost track of the greats and the great-greats, and there is no use trying to keep score as the numbers change as babies are born, people marry, divorce and re-marry, and some die. As can easily be imagined in a clan this large there is a grand diversity. Some doctors, some lawyers, a Playboy Bunny, a Flamenco dancer, sheep and cattlemen, superb horse people who compete in rodeos, a few folk who have been in jail, some counselors, an airline executive, bankers, musicians, builders and anything else you could imagine--suffice it to say there is always drama and excitement.

Almost everyone married, some unfortunately, some very well. Briefly, the sad ones were Donald, who married delectable Penny when she was only sixteen. She left him and their children to become a Playboy Bunny, and then she ran off with a rich doctor. The children have problems, of course. Donald's second marriage has been successful, and the two children from that union are doing well.

Yvonne married a tall, handsome policeman who got busted for running drugs. She left him. The children from that union have a few problems, too. Josie and Laura both somehow ended up with "difficult" men. Laura divorced and has lived a good life with her three outstanding children. Robert married a beautiful, charming Mexican and lived happily until he died, in spite of the coolness his Bertha endured from the racist elders. Julio and Rudy married great girls, and Glady captured, or was captured by, Lloyd, whom I have named Saint Lloyd, he is so great, as are their children.

There have been tragedies. Car and truck crashes took two, and left two more with brain injuries that have been challenging. Cancer killed three. Aids took one. One died of a heart attack. The elder Echeverrias have sailed off to The Great Beyond, wherever that is, from old age. Some have been to rehabs. Someone in the Echeverria clan gets to write all this down in an Echeverria family memoir that will be huge and amazing, but not I. The memories I offer here are enough.

Painfully disappointing to Miguel and Vicencia only one, their eldest son, Mikel, managed to marry a Basque. Mary Eraso was lovely, and a tennis champion at St. Mary's school in Phoenix. She was from a devoutly Catholic, respected Basque family. Dom had wanted to marry her. Mikel had rheumatic fever and was ineligible for the draft during World War II, so he stayed home when Dom went off to the Navy.

While he was gone, Mikel won Mary, and Dom grieved his loss over the years, lamenting to me often. Her cherry pie—I learned to make a killer one. Her brown eyes and black hair—no luck there. Strange but true, I felt genuinely sorry for my husband, and did my best to make up for his sad loss. I could not be jealous of Mary because she was truly wonderful. We all loved her. I accepted the fact that my background and my lack of the many skills the Echeverria women had, made it hard for Dom to understand me. Surely it was as difficult for him to cope with me as it was for me to cope with him.

When I met him, I was eighteen and had never known anyone like Dom Echeverria. The men on Remuda who pursued me, or whom I pursued, were gentlemen, respectful and decent, mostly. Dom was a powerhouse. When he walked into a room, the whole place vibrated. He was not a gentleman, and though I tried to be a good girl, and managed to be for the first year of our courtship, I finally stopped being good in a sand wash outside Tucson. There followed a thrilling, sometimes dangerous passion that lasted until he was killed twenty-three years later. Now, in the wisdom of my years, I realize that his disregard for my safety, his passionate insistence as he seduced me in my mother's liquor closet and the back of his pickup truck were danger signs. But back then, my objections added to the excitement and I couldn't help loving it. Meanwhile, my sorority sisters watched in awe. My mother urged me to leave him. His family wondered what he saw in me. All I could think about was that beautiful man who loved me so wildly.

My Mom, my brothers, cousin Bill, Dom, and I took a trip to

the Supai Indian Reservation, deep in the Grand Canyon. I hoped it would be a chance for Dom and my family to realize we were all mutually tolerable. An old, abandoned mine very high in a canyon wall, reachable only by an iron ladder with wooden rungs that had long ago rotted out, challenged Dom, and up he climbed. For a stretch just below the opening to the mine tunnel, four or five hundred feet up, the cliff leaned out so that he was almost upside down. We watched, terrified as he climbed, totally indifferent to the danger. He disappeared into the mine tunnel, and I wondered if he would meet some dreadful end there, but he emerged, climbed down, and said the tunnel was empty.

We were impressed with his bravery and athletic ability. The Supais were, too. They loved this dark, funny, lively man. Reed Watahomagie said in his Supai lilt, "Hey Dom, why you marry that ugly girl?" Dom said, "She's pretty nice even if she is too pale." Reed may have hoped Dom would gather up one of their lovely little princesses.

The trip did what we hoped. Dom's camp experience was helpful, his wit was as outrageous as ours, and we created wondrous adventures together. Even my mother grew to like him.

Many years later I became a counselor, first working with addicts of various varieties, and then with deeply wounded people. Among the many discoveries that came my way was a revelation about relationships and red flags. When lust gets one in its delicious clutches, and what seems like love, if not real love itself, thickens (or sickens, as my son Paul said) the plot, forget red flags. We simply do not pay attention, as I did not. Hope springs infernal (as my son Joe said). We seem trapped in the delusion that love will conquer all. Sometimes it actually does, but all too often, all it does is add poignancy and pathos to that sick plot. All the onlookers can do is sigh big sighs and stand by. When the "If only I had seen—I should have known—How could he, or she," moans begin, there is nothing much to say but, "Yeah, yeah, yeah, and what else is new?" I advise the sufferers to do what worked for me, go sit somewhere and be just as miserable as they can be until they get sick of it. Then it is time to get up, start "smiling no matter how happy we are," like Mortimer Snerd, and get on down the road. The thunder and lightning clashes created between Dom and me were terrifying and painful, but somehow love and yes, lust, kept getting me on down the road, and what a pay-off there has been!

Top photo: Dom's mother, Vicencia, holds daughter Josephine and son Mikel. Vicencia is around 20 in this photo. Bottom: Dom's father, Miquel.

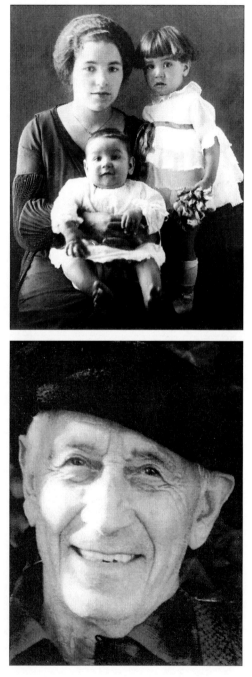

Top photo: Dom and his borthers and sisters. Back row, L to R: Roy, Robert, Mikel. Josephine, Dom (Domingo) and Laura. Front row, L to R: Rudy, Glady, Yvonne and Julio. Bottom: Dom's graduation picture from Wickenburg High School, 1943.

Top: The Echeverria brothers in the late 1940s. Their mother, Vicencia, called them "Los Bandidos." L to R: Robert, Rudy, Dom, Julio and Roy. Bottom: Dom as a Navy Air Corp Cadet.

Top: 1947 gathering at the Huntington Hotel in Pasadena, California. L to R: Dallas and Edie Gant, Remuda manager and hostess; Fred Wharton and author Sophie Burden; John Burden. Writes Sophie: "Fred Wharton tried to woo me by singing. Didn't work." Left: The author's college freshman portrait for Kappa Alpha Theta at the University of Arizona, 1946.

Top: New Year's Eve at Remuda, 1948. L to R: Dom, Sophie, and Roy Echeverria. Right: Sophie and Sydny Baker modeling for "The Bustle's" fashion show, 1946.

188

A Scandalous Soirée

Our wedding day was May 1, 1948, at St. Anthony's Church in Wickenburg. As the senior family member, El Scumpso was to give me away. He was a 32nd degree Mason, and refused to have anything to do with abominable Catholics or to set foot in a Catholic church. Nano was in fiery agreement, saying, "What a disgrace to have that Catholic join our family!" She carried on, finally ending her diatribe by imperiously announcing, "You know, Jesus was not a Catholic. He was a Jew!" "Thanks a bunch, Nano. Who would have guessed," was what I thought, but I managed to not say it. Uncle Pete and my brother John stood by in case Scumpso really balked, but at the very last minute, he appeared, scowling, to take my elbow and lead me into the jaws of perdition. Perdition or not, the service was beautiful, the church packed with family and friends.

A reception that is still famous followed at Remuda. The big living room was banked with Yuccas in full bloom, a band was playing, and everything was gorgeous. Everyone was eager to celebrate. Dom's aunt Tia Binancia's Buick ended up in our swimming pool and the assistant manager of the ranch ran off with a lady in a "borrowed" ranch truck that wasn't found for three days. They had stuck it in deep sand in the Powderhouse Wash. At dawn they hiked back to the ranch, red of face. One of Dom's brothers, whom I will kindly not name, had a fling with the church organist. Other scandalous things happened, too numerous to tell.

We gladly invited all of Dom's family, some 250 strong, and Remuda's friends and staff, another 250. Mom could not afford a dinner that huge, so the wedding was at 7 p.m., presumably after dinner. Cake and champagne were to be served at the ranch. We did not know that Basques never, ever do anything without food, glorious food. They raided the ranch storerooms and walk-in freezer and cooked everything on the place. It was a grand reception, and the food was delicious. The next morning my mother said all they had for breakfast was some wedding cake and champagne that had been left out on the patio. There, in the morning sun, stood twenty-two ranch guests up to their knees in bottles, cups, napkins, plates and all the trash of a spectacular party. Finding nothing to feed them, Sophie dashed off to town to beg for bread, bacon, and eggs from Wickenburg's three restaurants, since it was Sunday and Brayton's store was closed. The guests all left rather unexpectedly, right after breakfast.

For our honeymoon we cruised the California coast, as both of us loved the ocean. We stayed in beautiful hotels, ate great food, went to zoos, and saw shows, but my delight was almost destroyed by Dom's driving. He was wild. I was terrified. His mantra was "When in doubt, step on the gas!" and that is exactly what he did. Often he chose not to stop at stop signs and he even sped through red lights. I pleaded with him, but he said, "Stop worrying! I have magnificent perception and fast reactions, and I always look both ways when I am going to break the law." My lack of confidence in his "magnificent perception" infuriated him and I quickly learned to hide my fear and keep my comments confined to the scenery. Somehow we survived two weeks of California traffic and arrived home safely, but I realized Dom Echeverria was going to be trouble.

Dom wisely said that we would never make it if we stayed in Arizona with our families, so we moved to Colorado. He was to finish his pre-med studies at the University of Colorado in Boulder. We moved into the married students' dorm, ate in the cafeteria and settled in to our new life together. I worked in a "chi-chi" clothing shop where I didn't make much money, but acquired a great wardrobe. Then I went to the business school at the University for a semester, so I would qualify for more than minimum wage. It worked, and when Dom went on to the College of Veterinary Medicine at Colorado State University, I was hired for a better job as a bookkeeper in a hardware store. But the nuts and bolts kept getting mixed up. What a mess! I got pregnant and retired just in time to escape being fired. All I learned served me well over the years, though. I was able to manage the business and office ends of our enterprises, freeing Dom to run the livestock end of it successfully.

Weird Revenge

Something happened just before we left Boulder that gave me a flash of wisdom. The memory was triggered when a friend ranted about a wrong that had been done to him. With my encouragement he was able to decide, after blowing steam, to let resentment go and let revenge be God's.

Dom and I had a basement apartment close to the University of Colorado campus. (My little dog came into heat, and for days dogs looked down on us from the windows up by our ceiling. I wondered what we had come to, to be looked down on by drooling dogs panting with lust). We had lived in the University dorms and eaten in the cafeteria for the first semester, so this was our first real home together. Excitedly I cooked our first meal, but it was late, and Dom was angry. I explained how I could not find a recipe to cook canned peas in my new cookbook, and certainly we would suffer if I did not figure it out. Dom laughed! He remembered the story about my poor mother and the ice water when she was a new bride. I had come by it honestly. Damn that DNA!

Soon after we moved in, I became pregnant and miscarried. My gynecologist made a house call and did what he could to heal my broken heart and the rest of me. Our landlord, Mr. Eden, was a "person of the lie," as described in M. Scott Peck's remarkable book by that title. We used to hear him abusing his poor little wife. She was not allowed to speak to us, and there was no way we could help her. Mr. Eden had spied on us and came storming down to the apartment, accusing us of having had an abortion. He was going to prosecute us and put our gynecologist out of business. Dom tried to beat him up, but he jumped in his car and escaped. Our doctor said, "There is nothing that little weasel can do, and since the semester has ended, and you are leaving for Arizona, just go." We never looked back.

We were so broke we could not even buy gas to get to Arizona for a summer job with the family. Palisade, Colorado, is blessed with grove upon grove of famous Colorado peach trees, and Dom spotted a sign announcing jobs picking peaches. We signed on, and moved into the migrant workers' living quarters, which were long, tin sheds. Our cubicle had bedsprings on the dirt floor. Luckily, we had packed our bedrolls. Our suitcases and clothes were piled in a corner. Off we went to the orchards, each of us with a basket for collecting peaches, my little Cocker Spaniel, Linda, following us. Dom proved to be their very best picker, and actually pulled in some money, as they paid by the basket. I, on the other hand, was among the worst; not only was I slow, I turned out to be allergic to peach fuzz. Doggone, it made me sick! I lay moaning on the bedroll on those damned bedsprings, my little dog beside me looking bewildered. Meals were served buffet style, and were geared to the migrant workers. Mostly beans and peaches, the food was pretty awful. I smiled my idiotic smile and tried to fit in. The women I tried to talk to scorned me. No way did I fit in. Holy s--t, I thought, this is what it is like to be the object of discrimination! I will never, ever discriminate against anyone again. (Except people who are evil. It is our responsibility to protect ourselves from evil.) Dom made enough money so we could leave, he could get to his better job, and continue on to the College of Veterinary Medicine. Now, back to the insight about revenge.

About fifteen years later we had five children who needed braces. Dr. Bell, our orthodontist, and I had become good friends, good customers that we were. (He finally gave me a discount.) One day he introduced me to his new office assistant and who should it be, but old Mr. Eden, in suit and tie, proud as a damned peacock. "Mr. Eden says you were friends when you were at the University of Colorado," said Dr. Bell. I bristled and shot back, "No, we were not friends at all." Mr. Eden slimed out, "Well, we had a little difference over the furnace in the basement." "No, you accused me of having an abortion and you threatened me with the law and my doctor with ruination." Dr. Bell gasped. I apologized to him, but said there was no way I was going to stand still for that snake to ooze on me. Dr. Bell fired him. Ah, revenge! But it was not sweet. It was icky, and blah, and ugly. Forcefully it was demonstrated that revenge is better left in God's hands, though for some strange reason, perhaps for the flash of wisdom, God dumped it on me that time.

Dom was not accepted by any of the medical schools to which he had applied. Right after the war, schools were swamped with returning veterans, and he had a C in German, and a minority name, which back then was a definite detriment. Secretly, I was relieved. Dom was rough. When he touched you, it often hurt. If anyone had a sticker, here he came with his pocketknife, probably straight from doing something with a sheep, unwashed, drawn like a saber. He dug stickers and ticks out brutally, telling his victim to "Shut up, it couldn't hurt that much!" I feared for any patients he would have, and was glad they would now be animals, which are vastly tougher. The College of Veterinary Medicine, at Colorado State University, accepted him and we moved to Fort Collins.

Creative Survival

We bought a small house with a basement apartment, close to the college. Dom borrowed $1500 from his parents for the down payment, which he quickly paid back. They announced for years afterwards that they had put him through college, a lie that was mystifying. Oh well. The apartment was rented to classmates the first year, and then to Dom's brother, Roy, who followed Dom in his quest for a degree in veterinary medicine. He brought his wife, Fawn, and their little children, Debby, Roy and Jody, with him. Impressively frugal, I managed to get both house and apartment furnished with "treasures" from garage sales and auctions. We couldn't afford much food, so I raised rabbits. I couldn't stand to kill them, as each was like my child, so when it became necessary (periodically we were staggeringly over-populated with bunnies, and we were hungry for meat), Dom stepped in, bothered not at all by any sentiment, to murder them. I went as far away as I could get, sat under a tree and cried. Then I went home and cooked them, with a lot of wine. Some of it got in the rabbit stew.

Dom had five years of the GI Bill, from his service in the Navy, which got him through the University of Arizona and the University of Colorado (two years in each), but after his first year at Colorado State University it was gone. We bought 246 old ewes with money I had from War Bonds and credit Dom secured from the Poudre Valley Bank. Farmers were glad to rent fields to us after they had harvested them, as our "old ladies" cleaned everything up, especially weeds, and they left great fertilizer. We moved them from one farm to the next for the following three years. Work was hard as we bred, lambed, sheared and marketed the lambs and the wool. An added advantage was the left over vegetables we slyly slipped home from the fields for free food.

Classmates helped gladly, as they shared the meat we produced. If anything looked as though it might die, we put it mercifully out of this world, and ate it. One spring, Dom sheared the whole band on an unusually warm day. So warm, some of the sheep were sunburned. That night a freak Colorado blizzard blew in, and they began to freeze to death, naked and sunburned as they were. The College dismissed Dom's class, and they rushed out to the farm and worked day and night to save as many as they could. Most did survive, thank God.

Running the sheep was so time consuming, I had to help Dom with the work and with school. He had me write and type most of his papers, and I helped him study. I held up bone after bone, saying, "Name this!" Little did I know how useful my new medical vocabulary would become.

During those four years, Elaine, Jack, and Peter were born in the

196

St. Vrain Hospital, in Fort Collins. We couldn't agree on a name for our first born if it was a girl. I wanted something beautiful, like Gabrielle, but Dom said it was bad enough coping with Echeverria, and favored Jane, or anything plain. While I was still out of it in the delivery room he named her Elaine after one of my most delectable sorority sisters, Elaine "Lamb Chop" Abbot.

Three weeks late, tiny Elaine (Lamb Chop?) was born with a lot of black hair and dark fuzz. When the nurse appeared in the door to present her to me for the first time, she looked at me, then at the baby, and said, "I must have the wrong room." Little Elaine was dark and furry, but she quickly grew out of it and has been beautiful all her life. When Scumpso, her great grandfather saw her, he said, "She looks like two burnt holes in a blanket, her eyes are so big and black." Her Great Uncle Pete said she was like an exotic flower and named her "The Peony Bush in the Garden" after a funny song the comedian Danny Kaye used to sing. Certainly she was Dom's child, dark and Basque, and he adored her.

Next came John Dana, whom we called Jack after my Dad. I suffered an abrupt placenta, and he nearly died. I prayed and prayed through that terrifying night and finally made a bargain with God. Unaware that God really isn't interested in bargains, I promised to become a Catholic, like Dom, if Jack lived. God must have laughed at me, but kindly.

Both God and I kept our bargain. Jack was alive, and cute as a bug, laughing and loving when he was not in distress, but something

197

was very wrong, and he was in distress a lot. The yellow pages directed me to St. Joseph's Catholic church and Father Tom McMahon began my instructions. He made them fascinating, though I could not go along with all of it. Finally, with an exasperated sigh, he said, "To find God in His Holy Church, you are just going to have to learn to be blindly obedient." "What? Me?" I responded, incredulous. But Fr. Tom and I had become such dear friends I blindly did my best for him.

Dom's qualities were impressive, but he thought only of business, sheep, or his college courses. It soon became clear that any intellectual or spiritual companionship I needed I would have to find elsewhere. Fr. Tom was the first of a long parade of priests and nuns who filled that void, not only with their bright conversation, but also with loving support. Thank you, Higher Power.

Jack was very ill from the beginning. No one knew what was wrong, and we went through doctors, hospitals, diets and treatments. Grandma Echeverria ordered us to take him to the good nuns at St. Joseph's Hospital in Phoenix. "They will know what to do," she said. The nuns snatched little Jack from me to take him for tests. He was terrified and I insisted I must stay with him, but Dom physically dragged me away. My heart was broken. Not just for little Jack, but because I realized that Dom would not defend his children nor would he be there for me. I was on my own. When we gathered Jack up the next day, whatever tests had been done told us no more than we already knew and Jack did not smile for two months. His trauma, his despair, his fear that he could be so readily abandoned by me shut him down.

198

He cried so pitifully that I almost never put him down. One night I didn't wake up when he cried, I was so exhausted. Dom put both of his feet in the small of my back and pushed me out of bed onto the floor, saying, "Go take care of your kid!" Devastated, I asked to go to Arizona with Elaine and Jack, to rest. Dom took my wedding and engagement rings, and any other jewelry that I might be able to hock, all my cash and my checkbook, and forbade me to leave. Nothing so nasty had ever happened to me, and I was devastated and terrified. Eventually, he let me go, and it may have saved my sanity and prolonged Jack's life.

My sanity was not helped much by a little drama on the train trip, overnight, to Phoenix. A young, nice looking conductor took pity on us and thought the best help he could give would be to seduce me. "What?!" I thought. What was it about me that attracted that? It is said that abused women, and indeed anyone who has been abused, develop a psychic V for victim on their foreheads and victimizers pick up on it and go to work. I was not that vulnerable, and I made it to Phoenix with my virtue intact. How wonderful it was to be met by John and taken home to Remuda.

We played in the sun. Wonderful Ed and Jane Havey, my godparents, where there to love us. The food was wonderful. The rest was divine. My gratitude is forever.

In a few weeks we returned home, terrified that without me to protect them Dom might have killed my little dog or our kitty, or our rabbits, but Fawn, my sister-in-law who lived in our basement, had saved them, bless her heart. I tried to provide little Elaine with all the love and normal life I could, while caring for Jack. There were many very good times: the Denver Zoo, lambs, bunnies, dogs, cats, and little cousins Debbie, Roy, and Jody. And, as is usually so with abusive men, Dom was just wonderful, for a while. He surprised me with a beautiful new station wagon, and he bought me Chanel # 5.

What Dom and I created between us was mysterious. Early in our courtship I realized there was something deep that God surely had a hand in, and I had better pay attention. After meeting my Theta Sorority sisters and the guests on Remuda Ranch, Dom thought he needed some polishing to reach his full potential. To my astonishment he asked me to teach him to speak a finer English, dress better and have nicer manners. This powerhouse of a man, this brilliant person, trusted me enough to ask. Lincoln School would be astonished, too, to learn how their polishing job on me spun off.

In return he taught me many of the Basque skills the Echeverria women had. One day he took me by the ear and forced my face down close to the bathroom sink. "Look at it!" he commanded. Never had it occurred to me that it needed cleaning. We had always had maids on Remuda, Aunt Billie had failed to teach me basic cleanliness and the Theta House had maid service. I just never noticed. Not only did he teach me to be aware, he taught me how to clean things up, which was a nice new skill. He also taught me to cook. Years later I served a fine Basque feast and he said, "My God, you are a better cook than my mother!" Well, I nearly levitated.

Best of all he extricated me, little by little from the mind-set instilled by my parents on Remuda. I was supposed to please, and if I failed, I would be ostracized. Dom saw people honestly for who they were, and he related to them honestly. No one was "schmoozing" anyone. How wonderful, how freeing it was to be that way in the world.

On a deep level we were creating each other. The friendship and the love that came out of that process enabled me to transcend his cruelty, and he was able to rise above whatever I did that annoyed him. Then there was the passion we were blessed with for the twenty-four years we were together. It was a splendid cement that closed the painful fissures his rage and cruelty ripped open and it made him forget I was blonde, with an under endowed chest, and that I was not Basque.

A Most Terrible Time

It was Christmas time so we left the ice and snow of Colorado and drove to Arizona. Jack, fifteen months old, became terribly sick. Dom's mother took one look at him and announced, "That kid is going to die." Shocked and scared, Dom took my arm and we left. We cried together over our poor little son. I had never seen Dom shed so much as one tear, and never again did he cry. Dr. Bralliar, our long-time family physician, believed only emergency surgery would save him. He lay crying plaintively in a hospital crib while I sobbed in the waiting room. Cruel rules prohibited parents from staying with their children. The surgical nurse brought him to me just long enough for one kiss and then she took him away. Crying frantically he reached his little arms out for me as she carried him down the hall to surgery. Since Dom was studying medicine Dr. Bralliar asked him to attend and possibly assist with the surgery. I went to the Catholic church where we were married and where I could be alone. The moment he died his spirit came to me. Sister-in-law Josie sat down in the pew beside me. I said, "I know. I know. I need to be alone." Quietly she left. We buried his sad, tiny self; his little furry toy dog snuggled beside him, next to his Grandfather Jack's grave.

I was devastated. Every day brought crying jags I could not stop, and little Elaine, broken hearted over the loss of the little brother she loved, needed more than I could give. Dom went out to the sheep or buried himself in school.

One day I left Elaine with my sister-in-law, Fawn, so I could feel the needed silence and solitude of St. Joseph's Church. Suddenly Jack was there. I could not see or hear him physically, but the reality of his presence was powerful and unmistakable. A transcendent joy, an ecstasy, overcame me. I felt as though I might levitate to the ceiling. Jack said nothing in words, but he conveyed a peace, a joy, and an assurance that all was well, all was very well, which is with me still.

Pete was born six months after Jack died, and it was soon apparent he had whatever killed Jack. There they were, the same dreadful symptoms, the vomiting of almost everything he ate, and a dreadful diarrhea. My blood ran cold. The disease identified as cystic fibrosis was diagnosed in Pete, and assumed to have been what Jack had. Genetic, a recessive gene carried by both mother and father causes the production of a thick mucous that clogs everything in the body. At the time, it killed its victims while they were still very small, as it did Jack. Over the years, research produced treatments and medicines that kept these children alive longer, until now some live into middle age. Pete was very ill, but he had a tenacity of spirit that kept him going full blast until he lost his fight at twenty-four. At the time Dom graduated with his doctorate in veterinary medicine, Pete was doing fairly well.

DEATH SCENES IN MUD AND SNOW

Our sheep prospered and when Dom graduated with his DVM he was able to buy a small farm near Berthoud, north of Fort Collins, where he set up his practice. The sheep hadn't done well enough to afford a real medical facility, so I was charged with caring for the small animal patients in our home. Dom quickly built a large animal practice, treating his patients, mostly cattle, on the farms he was called to. Many of the farmers in north central Colorado were German Russian, and they could not say Echeverria, instead stuttering out "Echiewadda, Echerinnia"—whatever. Dom settled for any pronunciation they could handle, they liked him, and his practice grew, but he did not like them much. He was constantly frustrated because those old guys would wait until their poor animal was almost dead before they called him. Then he would have to wrestle around in manure-laden snow or mud to try to save its life. Usually it was too late, the critter died, and the farmer refused to pay because Dom had not been able to cure it.

Fortunately, there were other farmers, ranchers and rural people who had horses and maybe a milk cow or cattle and a few sheep who became good clients and good friends.

One day a little cat arrived that had been slammed in a car door and was comatose. To protect her from toddlers Elaine and Pete who longed to comfort her, I put her in a cotton-lined shoebox in the middle of the dining room table where she spent her last two weeks. We called her "Center Piece." She died peacefully, never regaining consciousness. It was so sad.

Then there was a baby pet skunk to be de-scented, that Dom had put in a large garbage can to await surgery. I was his assistant, and while we scrubbed up, two-year-old Pete took pity on the little fellow, thinking he must be lonely in that big can, and climbed in with him. It took weeks of tomato juice baths to de-scent Pete. It gained us fame of a sort, as the local newspaper thought it was a tale worth telling. The skunklet thrived, was adorable, and his owners were delighted.

To let cystic fibrosis have its way with our family was unthinkable, and I was determined to have a healthy child to keep Pete and Elaine company, especially since Pete might not live long. Dom was not as daring as I was, but thanks to Catholic birth control (which I sort of practiced with blind obedience), I was soon pregnant. Paul popped out so easily I thought, "Hah! This is how to do it!" Paul was beautiful, dark, and perfect. As he grew, he turned out not to be quite so perfect, and he earned the name "The Terrible Tempered Mr. Bang." But here he was, a delight to all, thanks to God.

Dom stocked our farm with sheep, turkeys, chickens, ducks, pigs, and a milk cow named Lolly Pop. I loved Lolly Pop because she wouldn't let me milk her. She was annoyed that I couldn't squeeze it out as fast as she could produce it as I sat there on the three legged milking stool, my head pressed into her warm flank, just squishing away. All that came out were insipid little squirts tinkling into the bucket. She often swung her head around to fix me with a stare of pure disgust. One of our sheepherders had to take over and then there was an abundance of milk. The cream, free of processing, rose to the top, thick and lovely. I made so much Crème Brulee and ice cream that we actually got tired of it.

Elaine, Pete, and Paul as soon as he could crawl, were in heaven. In addition to our usual dogs and cats, they had all those other critters to play with. Elaine, four years old, grabbed a turkey by his tail feathers. The turkey took off in a dead run, Elaine held on, flying through the air between bounces, squealing with delight while the big bird squawked with consternation. After that, he was smart enough to stay out of her reach, though she did not give up trying. She was a huntress; she chased, he squawked, and around they went.

The pigs were great for garbage disposal. At dinner one night, Dom began griping about a pot of beans I had cooked. They were not like his mother made. I grabbed the pot and made a dash for the pigs. Dom, astonished, got up to follow yelling, "Stop! Stop!" I outran him, dumped the terrible beans in the pig trough—to their delight, (they loved me) and turned triumphantly to face a shut down Basque. That was a case of sweet revenge, so there are a few exceptions to leaving it to God.

Of course we still had our band of old ewes. When they lambed there were often twins, one of whom would sometimes be rejected, or there were problems and a lamb would be orphaned. Goats supplied milk, and the children and I fed the little orphan "Bums" as we called them, out of bottles.

One of the goats had a kid that was so adorable she became a beloved pet. Pretty Pansy was brown and white with mischievous, bright eyes, a lively tail that she shook to express exactly how she felt and a soft little bleat that was totally disarming. She slept with the children, played with them and our cats and dogs, dancing, prancing, and then cuddling up for naps. At meal times she would go from chair to chair, sticking her little nose up imploringly between us for whatever treat she could cadge. One morning she slipped in the kitchen door, went bound, bound, bound and landed on the table with her two front feet in two bowls of oatmeal. What aim! What a mess! Then she stuck her head in the refrigerator, too quick for any of us to stop her, and inhaled a leaf of lettuce. She began to choke. Frantically we tried to help her as she struggled for air. Where was Dr. Echeverria? No one knew. The next nearest vet was gone too, so I called the children's doctor, Don Arndt. He was there in five minutes and saved Pansy. He paused as he began to log the call in his black book and said, "I'm putting this down as a cardiac case. Your children's hearts were about to be broken."

For all the fun of it, and there was a lot of fun, it was extremely difficult. I could barely keep up; weeds suffocated our beautiful, big garden, and children outgrew clothes before I got around to ironing or mending them. I took care of all the office work, and sometimes as it piled up frighteningly, I agonized over what important task I might have let slip through the cracks. Dom took mercy on me and hired a lovely Mexican girl who came in once a week to clean, but by lunch the next day, you couldn't tell she had been there. Chaos reigned. One day the phone rang and a man, who sounded very important, asked, " Would you like to move to Peru?" "Indiana?" asked I, not able to remember where Peru was. "No, South America!" "Yes!" I replied, without a thought in the world beyond escaping my work load on the farm.

He was from the State Department and he offered Dom a position as a ranch management advisor in President Eisenhower's Point Four Economic Development Program for Latin America. With a life history of ranching, a degree in veterinary medicine, and fluency in Spanish, Dom was their man. The job was prestigious and fascinating and Dom grabbed it. I was promised a house in Lima with a garden full of roses and all the servants I wanted so I could take wonderful care of my little children.

The farm was sold, Dom closed his practice and sold all our livestock except a band of superb ewes, "the Montanas" they were called, since they originated there. He shipped them to his brothers in Arizona to care for until our return. There was some sort of arrangement where they were compensated by keeping lambs and selling wool. I found homes for our cats and my beloved little cocker spaniel, which was the hardest part of the endeavor. Their faces, their pleading eyes as I said "good-bye"—Good heavens, my heart broke.

Just after Christmas I packed the house in preparation for the move to Peru. The government was to pay for transport of all our furniture, household goods, and even for our station wagon. I also had to plan what we would need for our trip to Remuda, where I was to have the baby I was carrying, due in late January, before joining Dom in Lima.

The realization that there was a large spread in age between Elaine and Paul, and without Pete, if he died, Paul would be sort of an only child, had been haunting me. Again, Catholic birth control worked and eagerly I awaited a new little person who I fervently prayed, and allowed myself to believe, would not inherit CF.

On New Years day, Dom invited some important business colleagues to our home for a fine feast to celebrate our new endeavor, and to close out, or put on hold, business we were doing together. All went well until, for desert, I began having labor pains. Conversation was lively and heated and went right on when I announced I had to leave. After a few more tries, I went out and sat in our pickup. Dom suddenly came to, and left his friends to take care of our little children, saying he would be right back. They all stood on the porch, waving, looking discombobulated. Dom stopped at a feedlot to check on a shearing crew and I thought surely the baby would be born there amidst a bunch of wool bags. I held out until I was on a gurney on the way to the delivery room. Dr. Arndt dashed in, just in time to see Anne Reed Echeverria

209

emerge, the first baby of 1956. "My goodness!" he said. "Holy s-t!" Dom exclaimed. I said, "I told you I was going to do it." I was too quick and silent for those fellows.

Dom dashed back to the farm to relieve our friends who were taking care of little Elaine, Pete, and Paul. Somehow, he quickly found a woman to babysit so he could return to his practice. He never confessed, but he may have picked her up on the side of the road. She alarmed him when he hopped in the shower and she pulled back the curtain for a good look. He got an emergency call and left, hoping all would be all right. She cooked fried potatoes, the only recipe she knew, which was just awful for little Pete's compromised digestive system. Dr. Arndt, ever my dear friend, intuitively thought he should check on the children, took one look and dashed to the hospital to drive me home. Anne was barely fifteen hours old. Holy Moley, what a mess!

I took one look and thought, "This is a witch." She had stringy, long grey hair, she was stooped over, she had a wart on her long nose and she radiated Evil. I could smell it. Dr. Arndt could, too. He said he was pretty sure she had escaped from a mental institution and he agreed about her witch-hood. The children were fascinated. Their Guardian angels hovered around, and all was well enough. Dr. Arndt and I got rid of her.

Dom was ready to leave for Peru, and the children and I were ready to fly to Remuda. The moving vans came and loaded everything swiftly, including Anne's formula, diapers, and everything I had packed for our flight, which I had hidden behind a door. "Good golly-miss-molly, what is wrong with you—gentlemen?" Caught myself in the nick of time there; I almost called them "stupid S.O.B.s." They had to unpack to find baby Anne's vital stuff. Our plane for Phoenix was scheduled to leave at 3:45, and it was past time to GO. In a cloud of dust we took off, the moving men still asking me what to do next, between comments that I was crazy and would never make it. Dom's wild driving got us there in the nick of time. The plane had to wait for us. It was warming up as we dashed across the tarmac. (In 1956, there were no jetways, You walked outside to the plane and climbed a set of stairs.) Dom's plane to Peru was to leave that evening. My mother and brothers met us in Phoenix, and took us home to Remuda.

Our two months there were wonderful. Help! Rest! Food I did not have to cook! Everyone loved my little children, and no wonder. They were adorable. The sun was warm, the family was fun, and the only dark cloud was Dom. He hardly ever wrote, and when he did, he reported that the job was interesting, the trips were enjoyable, and in Peru all the girls flirted with him because most Peruvian men were bald at his age. I began to worry.

212

Opposite page, top: Sophie and Dom at their engagement party at Remuda Ranch, 1947. Bottom left: El Scumpso leads Sophie into "the jaws of perdition," the Catholic Church. Writes the author: "No wonder I look terrified!" Bottom right: Sophie and Dom, just married, leaving the alter of St. Anthony's in Wickenburg, May 1, 1948.

This page, top: Wedding gathering, L to R: Aunt Clementine, bride Sophie, groom Dom and Echeverria brothers Mikel, Roy and Robert. His sister Laura, mother Vicencia and sister Josephine are in front.

Top: Sophie and Dom with son Jack and daughter Elaine at Remuda Ranch, Christmas 1952. Right: Daughter Elaine, age 1.

Opposite page, top left: John Dana, nicknamed Jack after Sophie's father, with his wooly lamb. Top right: Jack at age 1. He died of complications from cystic fibrosis three months later. It was the only time Sophie saw Dom cry. Bottom: Dom at his graduation from Veterinary School in Colorado, 1953.

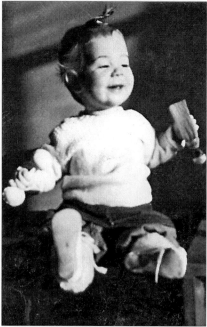

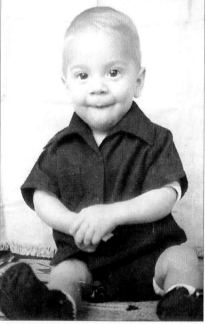

Top: The farmhouse in Berthoud, Colorado, where Dom started his veterinary medicine practice. Right: Son Pete, about 1. Also born with cystic fibrosis, Pete died at 24.

Opposite page, top: Elaine sits atop Buck while Sophie adjusts the stirrups in preparation for a horse show at Remuda Ranch. Bottom left: Elaine packs herself inside her father's suitcase, hoping to go with him. Bottom right: Son Paul, nicknamed "The Terrible Tempered Mr. Bang."

Top: The Echeverria family at Remuda
Ranch, just before leaving for Peru, 1957.
Sophie holds baby Anne. L to R are Paul,
Elaine and Pete. Right: Elaine, circa 1955

PERU

One day Dom called from Lima to say he had found a pension where we could stay, and that I was to come. We were supposed to leave on March 25, 1957, but on the 24th, Paul had a fever of 105.5 degrees. Criminy, what next! He revived, and off we flew on the 28th, my dear family looking concerned and crushed. They may have thought they would never see us again.

The airline did not think they could handle us, and I had a real fight with them to let us go. For twenty minutes I argued, while the big airliner sat there waiting for us. I won. We changed planes in New Orleans and once again they decided I was all mixed up, and shouldn't be flying. When we finally were allowed to board, little Elaine, five years old, said, "Mommy, I was so embarrassed! I thought you were going to sock that man in the jaw!" I think the man did, too, because we were given a private section all to ourselves, no doubt, he thought, a kindness to the other passengers.

There was a long layover in Miami. I hailed a cab to take us somewhere other than the terminal. The driver, surely another angel—they turned up all the time—had just become a first time father, and he wanted our little group to TEACH him things. He took care of us all day. Off to a beach we went, where he sat in the shade with tiny Anne while the children and I waded in the surf, finally falling in, "airplane clothes" and all. The ocean was irresistible. In the warmth of Florida, we dried out fast, and made our plane only slightly rumpled.

The government provided us with first class tickets so that berths could be made up for the overnight flight. We pressed our noses to the windows, looking out at an ocean vast and dark, sprinkled with island lights now and then, echoing the sparkle of stars we almost touched. A full moon rose, frosting floating clouds with silvery light. Our berths with white sheets and soft pillows were deliciously elegant, but we could hardly sleep. We were going to PERU!

Dom had been working with the Point Four Economic Development people, devising plans to best address the lofty aims of the program. With the enterprise went a whirlwind of socializing. The families of the Point Four personnel were all living in Lima, in fine homes paid for by the government, doing a great deal of partying. They shunned the Peruvians, except for a few wealthy or important ones. To Dom, this was not what Point Four was about, and it would earn us enmity rather than cooperation with Eisenhower's vision. He asked that we be stationed on one of the Granjas (ranches) instead of in Lima, and one of the largest, Granja Porcon, was chosen for him.

The house there was deemed inappropriate for the new "patron" with his American family and a Peruvian crew was sent to update it. While Dom waited for its completion, he lived in a pension in Mira Flores, an elegant part of Lima. Two middle-aged, single women owned it, and they doted on him. The three of them played cards every evening, and watched Peruvian soap operas. It was not until two days before I arrived, and Dom rented a cottage in the back garden for us, that they found out he had a family. The ladies must have felt betrayed, certainly they were angry, but Dom had gotten around their dislike of children and had manipulated them into a lease; signed and delivered, there it was.

Dom met us at the Limatambo Aero Puerto, striding across the tarmac, looking like a movie star. I had tried to look like one, too, but he greeted me with, "What happened to you? I'm really disappointed." (What did he expect after a trip like that?) Nonetheless, after he checked us into our cottage in the pension garden, warning us to drink only bottled water, he pulled me into our bedroom and made instant love, over my objections that the children were loose.

Indeed, Paul had found a cup and was drinking out of the toilet. He felt no ill effects. Somehow we settled in. The little cottage was nestled in a back corner, enveloped in flowering vines and greenery. The children raced around, delighted. We appeared for dinner in the lovely pension dining room. The ladies greeted me with scorn and icy daggers. I hoped it would be better with Dom's colleagues and I think it was, but I am not sure. At an introductory luncheon in a restaurant

221

downtown, we were seated in the patio garden with Dom's boss and several colleagues. Flowers arched over us in vines and burst out of beautiful urns surrounding us. Dom was splendid in his gabardine pants and white shirt and tie. I wore a turquoise dress with white lace collar and I looked like the perfect, lovely little wife. There is a picture of me to confirm it. All was going well. I commented in my fractured Spanish that it was hot, which it was, but what came out was that I was "passionately aroused." Dom kicked me hard under the table and told me not to speak Spanish anymore. The men laughed, bless their hearts. They may have thought Dom was really lucky to have a hot wife like me, but all he could think of was how I had embarrassed him.

Dom left for Argentina. The children and I had nothing to do but hike around our neighborhood. I hired taxis to take us to a museum and a park, but mostly we were stuck. Then our station wagon arrived in Callao, the shipping port near Lima, and the children and I excitedly took a cab to get it. We had wheels! We were free! Driving in Lima was terrifying until I figured it out. Most streets were narrow, often cobblestone, and one-way. Horns were prohibited, so everyone drove with windows down, pounding on the doors and shouting at each other. No one was hostile, just noisy. At night, we all drove with our lights out so we could flash them instead of honking. The one-way streets were rarely, or obscurely, marked, and the Policia stopped me frequently. They thought I was too young to drive, that I was a babysitter, a cute blonde with adorable kids. I never got a ticket.

I was given a map so I could memorize all the one-way streets in that city of over a million. With the help of the map I found wonderful museums that had Inca gold intricately etched with exotic designs. There were pottery vessels depicting Inca life, and paintings done by the Spaniards, mostly of suffering saints and Christ's crucifixion depicted as gruesomely as could be imagined. That seems to be a Spanish thing, as in Spain the museums have not much else. We were denied entrance into one gallery. I finally got it, with my limited grasp of Spanish, that it was all pornography. The history of Peru was fascinating and I found books in English that told of the magnificent Inca civilization, and of the fatal flaws that made it possible for Pizzaro and his conquistadores to destroy it utterly. As fascinated as we were, we had to stop going to museums because Paul and Pete were not exactly scholarly in their attitudes towards the artifacts. In fact, we were asked to leave rather forcefully the last time we tried it.

We fared no better when we tried to go to Mass in a cathedral. The children were so "lively" they would surely disturb worshippers, so we sat in the back. I soon noticed all the women were in front, heads covered in mantillas or scarves, and their men were in back, mostly standing. We were scowled at. How could a mere woman be so bold as to be hanging out back there with the fellows?

Dom returned from Argentina with tales of Punta Arenas, where the houses are painted wonderful, bright colors, perhaps to dispel the gloom of the cold and misty climate. He told stories of a band of Indians, nearly wiped out by the Spaniards, who dove for pearls, food, and treasure off the icy coast. They lived practically naked in near

223

freezing temperatures, and could stay underwater for three minutes. He shared tales of elegant resorts on the Atlantic coast where Point Four colleagues entertained him along with local men of importance. A large, wealthy ranch hosted him lavishly near Buenos Aires, where he selected rams worth thousands of dollars to upgrade their breeding stock. There were trips through the Pampas, where he rode over endless grass plains on sturdy ranch horses that could gallop all day. At night there were campfires, around which knowledge, culture, and plenty of wine were shared. They slept on the ground, or in tents if it rained, and Dom was grateful for his upbringing which made it all familiar and easy. The paintings he brought back of gauchos swinging their bolos and breaking wild horses told vividly of a vibrant, rugged culture. Carefully, he avoided politics, as instructed by the government, and said little about the injustices and abuses that were endemic. He just taught them how to run their operations profitably, and success was his in that.

When he breezed into Lima between assignments, he hired Cholo girls, natives, to care for the children while we attended dinners and business lunches with his colleagues, both American and Peruvian. The food was wonderful, the company delightful, but it was also distressing to me. When we left those elegant restaurants children were begging on the streets. They lived there, sleeping on benches or under trees, possible because it never, ever rains on the coast. I squirreled away all the leftovers I could and gave them to those hungry little people, but it was so little for such great need.

After one dinner everyone bid us good night and left. Dom just sat there. To my horror, I realized he was so drunk he couldn't get up. We had been drinking Pisco Sours, a delicious, delectable, disastrous mix of Agave, egg whites and sugar that sneaks up on you. With my broken Spanish, I managed to get waiters to help me hail a cab and drag him into it. When we got back to the pension, the bellboys unloaded him. He said, in the morning, he feared he might be like his brother, Mikel, who was a destructive alcoholic, and after that he almost never drank. The few times he did, he was terrifying, so surely his fear was right on.

Legends of Splendor

There is a legend telling of an island in the middle of Lake Titicaca, the highest lake in the world at over 12,000 feet, so large you can't see across it and bitterly cold. This island miraculously was host to tropical vegetation and a benign climate. There is a deep cavern there, in which are hidden golden tablets with writing left by the first Incas who arrived on a brilliant ship that came from the sky. The Aymara and Quecheua Indians, inhabitants of that lofty land, tell of it, and say that the huge markings on the plains at Nasca were to guide the glowing airships. The legend describes the magnificent, fair-haired, blue-eyed first Inca and his beautiful consort as sailing from the island to begin their conquest and rule of Peru and much of western South America. Later, during Pizzaro's despicable conquest of Peru, the Indians realized that the Spaniards' lust for gold was overwhelming, so

225

they cleverly began taunting them with tales of incredible treasure, leading them on wild goose chases. Could they have hoped to lure them out on icy Lake Titicaca in search of the miraculous island and its stash of gold, to sink in their own greed? The island seems to have disappeared, and the golden tablets are lost, as is the way with most golden tablets. Moses lost his and Joseph Smith seems to have misplaced the Mormons'.

It is a mystery how the ancient Peruvians devised the esoteric markings at Nasca, and it would seem extra-terrestrials had to have had a hand in it. Yet there is a theory that they are markings to direct and cajole the gods to send rain to the desiccated land, but how they did it remains unknown, seems impossible, and it didn't bring rain.

I longed to go to Machu Picchu, a retreat built by the Incas in an impossible place on a precipitous mountain in the middle of practically impenetrable wilderness. The magnificent craftsmanship and architecture, the huge stones somehow lifted and fitted together intricately and immovably, and the sophistication of the whole plan intrigues me, and everyone who hears about it. Yet, with my little family, there was no way. My daughter Anne made it in 2000, and tells of spirits and mystical experiences she was given when she climbed to the top alone. It is a holy place.

When we first arrived, I asked Dom why he hadn't written, and he said, "Gee, Soph, I was afraid if I told you about everything you wouldn't come." Every day in Lima some new fact would come to light that was daunting. Obviously there would be no lovely home with roses on the patio, and no servants. He would be away most of the time, and our four little children, five and under, and I would be on our own. We had been through enough together that I was insulted that he thought me so lacking in courage, but at the same time I wondered if that courage would hold up.

One night a friend told me that when there are earthquakes, not unusual, be sure to jump to the front door and open it so that the shaking won't jam it and trap us. Just a few days later we had one, and I got that door open plenty fast. Another friend told me that when they have revolutions, be sure to stack mattresses in front of the doors and windows so that the bullets could not come through, and keep plenty of food on hand. Gunshots rang out in the night sometimes, but no real revolution happened while we were there. Our pension was enclosed in a high, adobe wall topped with broken glass, and we felt safe enough.

Dom continued to travel, telling of people he met, ranches, farms and estates he visited, and meetings he attended. He was moving in important circles, doing impressive work. He had become a man of considerable prestige. I didn't mind that he was gone so much, as what he was doing was so valuable that I felt honored to be his patient and resourceful wife.

He instituted programs of immunization and parasite control to cut death losses, and he introduced the concept, amazing to the Peruvians, that they could, through new strategies and management, produce finished beef, pork, and lamb. They had imported their upscale meats for hotels and restaurants from packers in the USA, while the meat produced locally was sold cheaply to the natives.

Argentina was an exception. Their beef was good, everyone ate it, and it was exported. While he introduced parasite control and some other management improvements with cattle, his primary mission focused on improving their sheep enterprises, in management, disease control, and breeding programs that would upgrade their wool production. All they had was carpet grade wool. With the introduction of Rambouillet rams, wool fine enough to be used for clothing could be produced. Dom brought us a picture of himself with an important Argentinean agriculture officer and a $2,000 Rambouillet ram he had imported for them. They all looked splendidly impressive.

The children and I, meanwhile, spent fine days at Lima's beautiful beaches. Agua Dura sported waves too big for us, so we just combed the beach, but Agua Dulce was gentle and we played happily in its little waves. Sometimes we drove into the foothills of the Andes, where we visited villages, ate in their street cafes, and got to know the land and the customs.

Several times we heard gunfire. "What is happening?" we asked. "Oh, when people get bored and disgruntled, and drink, they have revolutions." Dom developed a theory that most Peruvians, in fact Latins in general, for whatever reason, do not develop emotionally beyond adolescence, and that is why their countries are so volatile. While it sounded arrogantly down putting, it did seem to fit.

Lima is beautiful, with impressive homes, wonderful parks, and flowers everywhere. I liked loading the children in the big, English buggy we had and exploring on foot. Several times men followed us home, and I was told it was dangerous to go out without a man to protect us. When we were followed, it would be entirely my fault for smiling. How Latin is that? Blame the ladies as the men seem to have an almost desperate need to be above reproach and an equally intense desire to seduce. Or rape. Several men wanted to buy little Anne, as they were fascinated with her blondeness. Latin men are aggressive. The ladies in the pension told me to lock my doors and stop touring around.

Pete bit the pension watchdog and the dog bit him back, and he had to have two stitches. We were told to confine the dog for observation, but the pension ladies would not allow their little dog to suffer so. It was suggested we sue them and have them arrested, and oh goodness, it was exciting. But of course we didn't do anything like that, and everything blew over peacefully.

Eileen and David Chase were a couple staying at the pension between assignments. He was an American mining engineer who worked for Cero de Pasco, the immense copper company that controlled much of what went on in Peru and the rest of South America. They had lived in mining camps in Chile, Bolivia, Punta Arenas, and other remote sites as well as in Peru. Eileen was Chilean, blonde, elegant, well educated and fluent in English. We became fast friends. I confided that I was feeling sort of cast off by Dom, who left me so much on my own with our little children. She told of the mining camps David had "dragged" her to, some at 14,000 ft., all remote, all populated with Cholo and Mestizo workers. Her attitude was that David admired her so much he knew she could cope with anything. What a concept! I adopted it immediately, and became a brave adventuress instead of a neglected "ugly American tourist," as Dom said the Peruvians called us. Eileen became my source of wisdom and my main support.

Granja Porcon

The children and I stayed at the pension until proper accommodations could be arranged for us in Cajamarca, the town nearest the ranch where Dom had been assigned. Then one day Dom cheerfully announced that we could not live in Cajamarca because the town was full of diseased, drunken Indians and rabid dogs, and besides, there were no houses with plumbing. So he arranged for us to live in the house right on the Granja, the very one they had been fixing up all along. I had been deluded to think we would have a house in town, but the thought of rabid dogs and drunken Indians made me glad that Cajamarca was but another delusion.

Dom came back from a trip to Northern Peru, full of news and excitement. The house on Granja Porcon was finally ready. The government had shipped our furniture and all our household goods up into the lofty Andes. All we had to do was gather our clothes, put the beloved station wagon in storage, and head for the airport.

Avion Fawcett, the airline that served Peru, loaded us into a plane so small I wondered if it could clear the high Andes. We roared out of

230

Limatambo Aero Puerto, catching air just before the end of the runway, gasp, and up we went into the foothills just east of Lima, brown and rugged. It never rains on the coast, and the only water available comes from the few rivers we could see below us that rush down from the mountains, creasing the barren land with swaths of lush green. Then forests began to appear, and our little plane flew so low over them it seemed the trees were brushing its underside. Liquid began to form on one wing, and I asked what it was. The pilot cheerfully said, "Not to worry, its just a little gas leak." No one else was concerned, and in fact the excitement left little room for fear.

We cleared one last high ridge and dropped into a wide, green valley. Cajamarca lay in the middle, red tile roofs bright against white and adobe walls, a river transecting it, looking like a place from another world which surely it was. Our plane circled a pasture, and Cholos ran out to drive the cattle off so we could land. We were met in the cow pasture by a wonderful brass band. Blasting horns and banging drums enthusiastically greeted presidential candidate Belaunde Terry who was on the plane with us. The children were thrilled! Dom had engaged Belaunde in conversation on the plane, so he was beyond cool, but what they had discussed I gathered was mostly political hot air.

Cajamarca was beautiful, but I could see Dom's point. We paused to buy some food in an outdoor market and caught fleas in just a few minutes. A huge, ornate cathedral graced the center of town, and we ventured into its cool, vast interior. Women, swathed in shawls, kneeled in prayer before icons of saints and the Virgin Mary, all richly painted and adorned with gold. In fact, there was so much gold that we were struck by the deep faith of the destitute parishioners that kept them from stripping it, a faith that had made it possible for the Spanish priests to have collected it in the first place. I hoped we would make it to Mass there someday.

The town was the northern Inca capital, populated by Indians and a minority of Mestizos. The Mestizos were a group that we quickly grew to mistrust. Half-breed, Indian and Spanish Peruvians, they were too good for the Indians and way below the Spanish. They were angry, devious, greedy, and cruel, and we steered clear of them. There were exceptions and Hernan Zunico was one. He was tall and gregarious with strange blue eyes. Quite a few Indians and Mestizos have blue eyes, thought to have come down from the Inca nobles who were, in legend, described as Caucasian or people from other planets. Perhaps they came from Egypt in balsa reed boats, as proven possible by Thor Heyerdahl in his balsa boat, Kon Tiki.

Hernan greeted us smiling a warm welcome and took us into town in the Granja jeep. The little jeep was loaded to overflowing with our luggage, the groceries, Elaine, Pete and Paul stuffed in back and Anne on my lap in front with Dom and Hernan. We started the twenty-five mile trip to the Granja. The road became narrow two-track and dirt after it left the cobblestone lanes of the city. It wound up along a stream between banks of geraniums, glorious red, pink and white, as tall as the jeep. Up, up we climbed into the Andes, immense, surprisingly smooth and very green. There were occasional rock outcroppings, and now and then a brave little grove of bushes and trees. Centuries of wood gathering had done most of the trees in. Indians were everywhere, herding flocks of sheep, goats, pigs, and an occasional cow. There was a lot of inbreeding which resulted in rams with four and even six horns. The pigs were so odd sometimes it was hard to tell them from the equally odd sheep and goats. They were all small, with short, sturdy legs, and lots of scraggly hair or wool of some kind or other. Women in multiple, full, brightly colored wool skirts and smocks, wearing round derby hats ubiquitous in pictures of South American natives, herded the animals along with barefoot children. The multiple skirts were piled on top of one another, as when they became too frayed, they just put a new one on. The older women looked spectacular with all that colorful wool swirling around them. They were small, with fine features and pleasant faces, a little like North American Hopis, but smaller. At 5'3", 110 lbs, I felt like a hulking, ugly, pale person beside their agile, dark, petite selves.

We crested a mountain ridge that seemed to be in the sky. It was 14,000 feet and I was very dizzy. We looked down into a beautiful, big, green valley, in the middle of which sat a cluster of white stucco buildings. Livestock grazed on the surrounding pastures, and there were fields of cultivated wheat and oats. Down we went, over that precipitous road, holding tight and praying.

We drove up to the Granja headquarters, our new home. The place was fairly large, horse-shoe shaped, with the wing on the left composed of bedrooms, a kitchen, a dining room for the crew and an office. There was a lab in which Dom was to conduct his research and demonstrations of scientific livestock management. It consisted of a shelf with two jars, one holding a lamb fetus and the other a bunch of liver flukes. Some lab! No matter, the Granja was so far away from civilization that not one person ever turned up to be demonstrated to. The wing on the right was a barn and storage shed. Our living quarters were in the center. The wings embraced a courtyard that turned out to be a perfect playground for the children. The Peruvians thought that since we were American, they should put a floor in our house, a fireplace and a cement bathtub big enough to float a canoe. (Which was never used because we had so little hot water and it was cold up there at 10,500 feet.) I later wished they had left the dirt floor, as the other floors on the Granja were. The ever-present mud was a constant problem for us. The natives just stamped it into their dirt floors and carried on unbothered. There were two bedrooms. The children's was heated by a kerosene stove. The men who installed it thought it would be a shame to waste all the warm air that went up with the smoke, so the chimney ended in a sort of attic. The initial firing up was nearly the death of us. Fumes seeped down, followed by smoke. Dom had a heck of a time convincing them that chimneys were meant to go OUT.

Maria and Uto, Quechua Indians who spoke no Spanish, only Quechua, brought me a chicken, and since I do not murder chickens, and since we were not going to swim in that bathtub, we made a lovely home for her there. Her name, we were told, translated into "Pretty Big Chicken." I added "Pretty Big Very Good Chicken " as she provided us with an egg a day and she was delightfully personable. Chickens are short on brains, but by God, they have personality.

The Indians had nearly killed the manager whom Dom was replacing. They had tried to drop a big boulder on his head as he slept, but he turned over just in time to save himself, which was a pity, as he had been torturing them. He hung them up in the barn by their thumbs, among other things. Dom put an end to that, and he was truly loved for it. I was alarmed, but I told myself that I would not let them get me down, and we would have fun anyway, though obviously it was going to be a challenge.

The fireplace was made of uncured stone, so it cracked when it was heated, and we had to make daring dashes past it as it often exploded and shot hunks of rock across the room with loud booms, crashing into the opposite wall. We needed the heat, so we kept it going, hoping the rocks would cure out. They did not. In the nine or ten months we were there, we never took our coats off, indoors or out. Sometimes, it hailed three or four inches deep! In a way, it was fortunate, as in that cold we really did not need baths.

Our cook stove was colorful tile with an ornamental steel top and grate, quite beautiful, but it was only for wood, and the only wood available was green eucalyptus. We singed our eyebrows as we learned to light it with douses of kerosene, which, if not done exactly right, exploded alarmingly. Over the sink was a grand window, six feet wide, which looked over the rushing stream that bordered our yard. A stone bridge crossed it, made by the Incas hundreds of years ago, artfully arched, all of perfectly fitted rock. The only Quechuan word I managed to learn in the time we were there was "rumichaca," which means stone bridge. Not too useful, but I liked it. Across the noisy little stream the Andes began their ascent up to the 14,000-foot ridges. Green grass festooned with wild flowers, sheep grazing, Indians herding them in their beautiful ponchos and great straw hats, brilliant blue sky and white clouds (unless it poured rain, which it often did) all made my kitchen window a window to majestic beauty and wonder. I loved it.

Dom left the sheep, horses, and cattle in the care of Hernan Zunico and his crew while he went on missions to Chile, Ecuador, Argentina, Paraguay and Uruguay. He wasn't sent to Brazil or to the Northern Coast, because he spoke only Spanish and Portuguese is spoken there. The children and I were alone, twenty-five miles over a nearly impassable road from the nearest town with no phone, a cranky old generator for occasional electricity, a two-way radio to the head office in Lima, and no way out. It was scary, but such an adventure, and so beautiful that we loved it. The Peruvian men were leery of me, the boss's wife, and they barely spoke, but the Indians, Uto, Maria, and their son Phillipe, took care of us. We became like family.

We had been told to pack all the medications and toiletries we would need, as there was no way to get them in Peru. A mistake was made, and the few tubes of Vaseline I had ordered turned out to be two cases of big jars. Perhaps a Guardian angel was involved, as that Vaseline was Heaven sent. The Cholos went barefoot, or wore sandals, in

236

spite of the cold, which was practical, because they didn't have to clean the mud off their shoes, but their feet had big, nasty cracks and calluses. I rubbed Vaseline on them, and their relief was wonderful to see.

Food was a challenge. We ate jackrabbits, Yucca roots, tough purple potatoes, and an occasional chicken (but not Pretty Big Good Chicken!) and some eggs. Elaine's sixth birthday rolled around and I baked her cake of cornmeal (ground on stones, just like our native Americans used to do), raw sugar, and native cocoa, unlike anything we had ever seen. It was some cake! Really chewy, with little rocks from the grinding, but the Indian kids loved it and so did we. Elaine was thrilled and the party was a delight. Along with the cornmeal, cocoa and raw sugar, we had some canned vegetables and tins of milk, but we were short of meat.

The Peruvian government had imported some Brown Swiss cows, hoping that they would do better in the high altitude than the in-bred Peruvian cattle. These were very fancy cattle, and guarded carefully, but one died. Dom was off on a trip, so there was no veterinary help. Uto and Maria rushed in, calling, "Senora, Senora!" and gestured for me to pick up the kitchen knives and a big bowl and follow them. I, and our four small children, as well as the other Cholo families who lived on the ranch rushed out into the pasture to where the splendid cow lay, quite dead. Expertly they dressed her out, saving her entrails, the fetal calf she was carrying and her beautiful, brown hide. We began carving strips of meat off to take home and cook and make into jerky. That meat looked delicious! We were all so hungry for quality protein that we just began to eat her raw, strip by luscious red strip, hard as that is to believe. When I remember that, it seems like a dream. My little children and I, Uto, Maria and their little children, and the ranch Cholo families, ate that Brown Swiss cow raw, out in the Andes Mountains. Thank goodness Dom wasn't there, as he never would have allowed it.

Pedro, a Peruvian unafflicted with the faults we disliked so much, and his wife Blanca, were hired to work on the Granja. Blanca took care of little six-month-old Anne so that Elaine, Pete, Paul and I could join Dom riding the amazingly rugged trails up into the Andes. He had a fine grey horse, and I had a little bay, gentle enough to allow me to have three-year-old Pete in front with me. Two-year-old Paul rode in front of Dom. He bought Elaine a precious little bay with white stockings and a white star on his forehead. We named him "Big Enough" as he looked like and had the sweet disposition of the beloved "Big Enough" who "raised" my brother John. The rides were spectacular. The trails climbed, winding steeply, from our fertile valley to a surrounding rim of mountains 14,000 feet high. As our horses took us higher and higher, they puffed, I puffed and prayed I would not get dizzy. We gained the top of a high ridge where the horses stopped for much needed rest. The Granja, thousands of hectares, so large it took four days to ride across, stretched before us on all sides. Our house sat in its surround of pastures far below. Mountains stretched to the west, towards Cajamarca, and to the east, the slope eased down into jungle. It took all day of hard riding to get down there, so only Dom and Elaine ever made it, but we could see off in the distance to the magnificent spread of it. We checked the bands of sheep that were grazing on the high pastures for injuries or illness, made lists of what the herders needed, and looked for cattle roaming the wild ridges.

Even though our horses were strong enough, Dom hoped to obtain some of the mules that were bred especially for the high Andes. Big sturdy Jacks were bred with Paso mares which produced mules with the smooth Paso gait but retained the strength and endurance so valued in mules. Take note of that gait in Western movies. Quite often, the hero will be astride a horse that rocks along so he doesn't bounce. A Paso cross affords an actor the illusion that he is a marvelous, "unbouncing" horseman.

Dom never managed to get the mules, but he did buy me a grey Paso stallion, one which had been shown and had won trophies. He was named Jerano, which meant a guy who played around a lot. When Dom finished his tour of duty and was to return to the States, he felt he could afford to bring only one horse, and unable to choose between Big Enough and beautiful Jerano he left them both. We cried. Both had good homes with friends in the Lima Hippodrome, (horse park) thank goodness. I wish he had brought the horses instead of so many Peruvian "treasures." Maybe not. Our beloved horses would have grown old and died, and we still have the beautiful leather topped furniture, the paintings, the silver and antique pottery juacos.

Heroism sneaked up and bit me on the rear, all uninvited, time and again, in Peru. Leaping lizards! That was one wild place! The children and I loved hiking the trails that led through the meadows up into the foothills. We topped out one day at a rock outcropping, and sat down to puff. (There was a lot of puffing in the high Andes.) Suddenly, from beneath the very rocks we were sitting on, a host of red and black scorpions, as big as cockroaches, emerged. They seemed to be attacking us! I gathered little Anne and Paul, and the five of us scrambled down the hill as fast as we could go. In the descent, Elaine grabbed some brush to steady her little self, and began to scream. I could find nothing that had bitten her, but her hands were turning bright red. I smeared them thickly with mud, as we had done on our adventures in the Grand Canyon, where we spent summers camping. Soft, thick mud sucks poison and soothes bites, and it helped Elaine enough so she stopped screaming and we made it home, well ahead of the scorpion army, and clear of the stinging nettle that had stung her.

Sometime later, I opened a can of Peruvian peas for lunch, and they frothed and bubbled, overflowing the can. I dumped them quickly, and turned to other things to feed us. Paul got in the garbage and ate the peas. For an hour and a half I did all I could to induce vomiting. It was ghastly. He never threw up a single pea, and I resigned myself to his imminent death. There was nothing to do. We were alone. No phone, no two-way radio, nothing. So we went on a picnic. It seemed the best way to spend his last hours on Earth. The more we hiked, the better he got, but even so, I crossed Peruvian peas off our list.

On Sundays when Dom was home, we piled into the Jeep, climbed up out of our beautiful, green valley, over the high ridges and down to Cajamarca. The drive was gorgeous, mountains so grand, so green, and everywhere small, dark, beautiful people driving their odd little bands of sheep, goats, and pigs. If any of us had to stop, there was no bush to go behind, and even if there was one, there would surely be a Cholo there, so we held on. Mass at the cathedral was our destination. Father Tom, back in Fort Collins, had told me that Mass was always said in Latin, as the Church was Universal, and the Mass would be the same everywhere. Indeed it was, there in the Inca's northern capital, and the sense of being part of its universality was exciting.

Early in my days as a Catholic I rewrote the Mass to suit my arrogant little self, as it seemed all wrong, universal or not. The church was selling God way short, I thought. The venerable Fathers had created a God in the image of man, and a cruel, petty man at that, instead of the other way around, as decreed. If I was to stay the course, which I intended to do, adjustments were necessary. The "Mea Culpa" had to go. I prayed, instead of whining about what no-good, unworthy sinners we all were, "Here we are, God, good people struggling to be ever better. Give us some help so we can serve You well." I sensed the Holy Trinity was far grander, kinder, and more benevolent than the church would have them. The passionate love Dom and I shared, which was surely a gift from God, led me to believe that Mary did not remain a virgin after Jesus was born. Scripture speaks of his brothers, and while I was instructed that "brother" was used in the sense of the universal brotherhood of man, I chose to take it literally, like Christians take most of the rest of the Bible. Why, how, could Joseph and Mary be de-

241

nied the beauty of a complete marriage? The vision of them as a holy, whole, totally loving family inspired my adoration far more than the Catholic version of a dry, frustrated union with Jesus an only child. So there I was, faithfully getting us all to Mass, while enthusiastically raising a tribe of heretics.

Elaine had her sixth birthday, July 6, 1957, so she was ready for first grade. The Calvert School for families unable to attend traditional schools sent her courses, and I began to teach. She was impossible. I could not figure out what I was doing that so enraged her. We were at war. Dom thought we should investigate the Catholic boarding school in Cajamarca. She would be safe with the good nuns, and her Spanish would be perfected. We arranged an interview at the convent with Mother Superior and the Monsignor who were thrilled at the prospect of a "rich" (they assumed) American student in their school. They fawned over us as though we were royalty. Obviously Elaine would be treated like a princess, the natives would hate her, and she would become even more imperiously contentious with me. That plan died. When we returned to the States, she would just have to muddle through first and second grades.

Dom had befriended Enrique Dobertin, a German immigrant who had moved to Cajamarca as World War II ended. He had married an elegant Indian woman, Maria, and they had a little, darkish blonde, blue-eyed daughter. They asked Dom to be her Godfather. Someone from Maria's family was the Godmother. Off to the Cathedral we trooped for her baptism. There was a line of Cholo families that extended out into the street and down the block. Enrique said, "They come from far and near, some of them walking for days to get their babies baptized. There is always waiting, sometimes for days, and it is a terrible hardship." Enrique enjoyed enough prestige that the priest ushered him in ahead of the poor Cholos and little Veronica was baptized, held by Dom, her long, white lace dress cascading over his arms, the dusky Godmother holding her tiny hand. Then the priest sauntered out and told the Cholos it was closing time, and they could come back tomorrow. Shocked, I asked what in the world that was about. It seemed the clergy had little regard for the natives, and did whatever they felt like doing on any given day. The Monsignor drove up and down the valley in his big, black Buick, demanding money from everyone. Enrique told of the death of the Monsignor's predecessor and of the funeral, grand and pretentious, during which his twenty or more illegitimate, half-Indian children turned up. In Peru, social and financial advancement could be gained by lower-class men only by becoming priests, so they flocked to church vocations. As for the nuns, they were escaping the slavery of arranged marriages and the grinding poverty endemic there.

There was a monastery of Mary Knoll brothers near Lima who were wonderful and who did good works, but the rest of the church was corrupt. Yet faith was powerful, and people kept coming, bringing all the money they could. Confused and disillusioned as I was, I was one of them, but we gave no money. We did all we could for the people on our Granja, and that was enough.

As always, I prayed. One day I was praying fervently, and God said to me, not audibly, but clearly and powerfully, "Soph, if you would just shut up a minute, I could get a word in edgewise." That is when I began "Listening," which actually was a form of meditation. What I have heard over the years since has been amazing to me. Miraculous. Almost always, just in time, I seem to know what I need to know.

We sometimes went to the Dobertine's for lunch or dinner. Enrique had built a lovely hacienda on the side of a hill, with red tiled floors and roofs and a veranda overlooking the city. Maria and their several maids turned out delectable food, Enrique spoke English, and those were times to relish. He confessed to Dom that he had been a submarine captain in the Nazi Navy and barely escaped the war crime trials after the war. He was hiding out! There were many Germans and Italians throughout Latin America hiding out. While it may have been a disgrace to "host" these people with such dreadful histories, they brought valuable gifts of skill and ambition that advanced those countries. The paradox gave us much to think about. War criminals, some like our friend Enrique, who may have done no more than obey orders, were now doing good in the world. We could not have done otherwise than to accept and value his friendship.

On those adventures to town we explored. The hot springs where Inca kings had bathed were considered holy and bubbled clear and lovely just outside of town. No one was permitted to swim in them. The town was graced with fountains, a few ornately decorated mansions, and many odd little shops. Our jeep was too small to take anything more than food back to the Granja, so we just looked. The children played around the fountains, climbed on statues, and made tentative connections with the native children. Then we would load up and negotiate the twenty-five miles back to our home.

The road followed, more or less, ancient routes taken by Cholos for centuries. Horses, mules and sandaled feet had dug the old trails so deep that they creased the hills in long, parallel ditches. Our road staggered along beside them.

THE INCAS

⁀

The ancient Incas' highway must have been somewhere near us.
They had built a road 2,700 miles long, from Chile up through Ecuador,
paved in stone brought from distant quarries. The Andes' steep sides
were negotiated by terrifyingly precipitous stretches carved into rock
cliffs. Somehow it crossed rushing rivers. Along the route were resting
places and temples to the sun where they worshipped. The Spaniards
wrote about them with awe and envy, declaring there was nothing like
it in all of Europe. The royal road kept the huge empire tied together,
the Incas' tight control extending everywhere, uniting the many di-
verse tribes into an imposed peace and order. Even marriages were
arranged. Freedom? It had been a destructive concept among many
small, warring tribes. Necessarily sacrificed, the Incas created a uni-
fied, tightly managed civilization of splendor and prosperity. We rat-
tled along in our jeep, imagining, dreaming what it had been like. In
the distance to the south, we thought we could discern a long inden-
tation in a mountainside that surely was a remnant. We scanned the

wild country, wondering where the Incas had hidden gold and silver when Pizarro conquered them. No one has found it. We hoped no one ever would, unless, of course, we uncovered some, which was a fanciful fancy.

What Pizarro and his conquering Spaniards did was so barbaric, so appalling, that any remnant of the Inca civilization should be honored as tragic and sacred and left to lie in the Andes. The Peruvians are doing this by preserving ruins and creating fine museums. The history is long and so complicated that if one is interested, one must do some research. I like to relate only the highlights gleaned from the books I managed to find in Lima, and what people talked about. Boiled down, the Catholic Spaniards came to convert the "poor heathens," but they were positively psychotic, in my opinion, split apart in mind and spirit, because much stronger than their holy quest was their incredible greed.

A strange combination of events and beliefs rendered possible the conquering of that magnificent and immense civilization by a small, grungy band of nasty men. Their horses overwhelmed the Indians who saw them as no less than god-like, and the guns that wreaked such sudden death terrified them. There were characteristics of the culture itself that rendered them all too vulnerable. The Incas believed in an ancient prophecy that Huyana Copac, the last great king, reiterated as warning on his deathbed. First, he named a favorite son, Atahualpa, as his successor, but then he warned that it had been foretold that after the twelfth Inca, and Atahualpa was the twelfth, the empire would fall. With that fatalistic belief on board, they were all too accepting of what they saw as their foreordained fate. They did not fear death as they believed that their "Great Sun God called them to his bosom to rest there in eternal joy." Huyana Copac had many wives and there was much infighting over succession among Atahualpa's brothers, too complicated to relate here. Suffice it to say that Atahualpa ended up ruling the northern provinces of which Cajamarca was the center.

Pizarro asked for a peaceful meeting with Atahualpa, who consented, but when he arrived, Pizarro was not there. Atahualpa was taken prisoner and locked in his own prison. He was served his meals on his golden plates, however, and the plan was to extract ransom. The Inca, unable to fathom such gross behavior, became terrified and bargained for his freedom by promising to fill the room he was imprisoned in with gold "as high as he could reach" and to fill the adjacent room with as much silver. From far and wide his people began arriving with the treasure. The priests whose mission it was to convert one and all to the Catholic faith, began preaching to Atahualpa, telling him, through what was surely rickety translation, what the Bible "said." The Incas did not have writing. They kept detailed records with "quipus," multi-colored cords, knotted in complicated ways which no one has been able to interpret. When the Spanish friar spoke of what the Bible "said," the Inca had no idea what that meant and held the Holy Book to his ear to "hear" the "said" message. He heard not a word and threw the Bible to the ground in disgust. In fury at such sacrilege, Pizarro, who was watching, hidden, yelled, "Santiago!" the call to war. Pizarro mounted his beautiful stallion, which had been trained to whirl and leap magnificently, utterly stunning the Indians into abject terror. With flashing swords the Spaniards swept into the crowds that had gathered, and in two hours, thousands had been killed, but not one Spaniard. They wondered at Atahualpa's resignation. Aware of the dreadful prophecy, the great king awaited his fate with dignity. To be burned at the stake was the sentence for the sacrilege Atahualpa had displayed, but he was much admired for the fine, intelligent man he was, and he was offered the much "kinder" execution of garroting if he would convert to the church. This he did, and he was strangled there in the square in Cajamarca.

Meanwhile, word had reached Atahualpa's best general, who still held Quito and its immense treasure. Ruminahui, faithful and brilliant, quickly gathered fifteen thousand warriors to carry sixty thousand loads of gold into the Llanganati Cordillera. Ruminahui had been born near there and knew where to hide the treasure where no one would ever find it. The Spaniards captured and tortured many in efforts to find the place, but no one knew the secret of its location. High in a perpetual fog, the Llanganati is a wild, razorback chain of mountains between the Amazon Basin and the Andes highest peaks and volcanoes. It was so ruggedly desolate no one could live there. When they neared the area where Ruminahui planned to hide the treasure, he sent all but fifty of his men away. The treasure was hidden in deep caverns by those few, after which the nobles led the men to a distant place, hung them all, and committed suicide. Unless they did not. Another tale says Ruminahui was captured, tortured in efforts of get him to reveal the location, and left burning alive in the square of Quito, silent to the end. The treasure is still hidden.

The Spanish, greedy bastards that they were, had the very artisans who had created them melt down the gorgeous artifacts into ingots of gold and silver to be sent back to the Spanish Queen. The few treasures that escaped tell of a lofty civilization capable of great art.

The Spaniards left the peoples of all of Latin America, from Argentina up into Mexico, with small pox. Millions died.

The history of the conquest of the glorious Inca Empire perhaps is a scenario, painted dramatically on a grand canvas that is echoed throughout life. Time and again I have found myself "done to" because I am so doggoned nice. "I'm just a girl who can't say,' NO', I'm in a terrible fix! I always say, 'Come on, let's go, just when I oughter say, NIX'," to quote Ado Annie in "Oklahoma." In a small way that is not unlike Atahualpa, who hoped for some kind of civilized rapport with the invading Spaniards that rendered him too vulnerable. Is there another echo brewing as President Obama seeks rapprochement with countries that openly loathe us? As Atahualpa was admirable for being open to Pizzaro, and as I am for being kind and generous, are Obama's admirable and hopeful overtures opening us to trouble? Think I'll have a beer and pray.

And Now, Back to the Granja

～

Indian babies began dying of "Tus Negra" around the Granja. Dom came in one evening, pale and shaken. "I rode over to a worker's hut, and out in the middle of the field on a big rock, laid out side by side, were two little twins, dead. I found their mother in the hut, sobbing, 'Tus Negra, Tus Negra,' utterly distraught." He didn't know why she had abandoned them there. Maybe she was trying to protect her other children. He said it was one of the saddest things he had ever seen.

"What is Tus Negra? What did they die of?" I asked Zunico, but he couldn't or wouldn't tell me. Dom was away again, so Zunico fired up the old generator that powered the radio to the head office in Lima. I asked and someone said it was small pox. Dark terror gripped me. Someone else came on and said, "No, it was whooping cough." What the heck did anyone know anyway? Anne was only three months old when we arrived in Peru, too young to be immunized. "Send DPT and small pox shots!" I said, and a few weeks later Dom arrived with a package that had never seen the inside of a refrigerator. He suspected it was ineffective, since it left little more than a pinprick on her arm, and we feared she was unprotected.

In the middle of the night a Cholo came banging on the door pleading for "El Doctor Dom." A young woman was trying to deliver a breached baby and they were desperate. Dom asked my advice. If he went, he might bring whooping cough back to Anne. If the young woman and her baby died while he was in attendance, he might be held responsible. He was a veterinarian, not an obstetrician. The thought of the little Chola out there in a mud and straw hut in agony was unbearable. To protect one's own, or to help a fellow human in distress? I thought of my little children and their agony if Anne caught Tus Negra and died, or if they lost their father to an angry tribe should the Chola die and they blame him. Distraught, I asked him not to go, but that decision haunted me. We prayed. In the morning, word came that she had delivered and was all right. Another miracle. But the baby was not doing well. Its tiny arm had been broken in the efforts to extract it, and the little mother could not have been well, either. What a hard planet it is that we are sailing through space on, and Peru was one of the hardest places. How strange a juxtaposition as it was also one of the most beautiful. There was nothing to do but keep on praying. Again it worked, and the young mother and her baby eventually were all right.

The Tus Negra came closer and closer. Indian children were dying all over the valley. The Cholo homes were small, thrown together affairs with dirt floors and roofs thatched in heavy Peruvian grass.

252

They barely held out the rain and hail, and were cold. Large guinea pigs, called Cooies, were part of every family as they slept with them to keep warm. They also ate them. Wood was scarce, so cow pies were often the only fuel for cooking, but they were inadequate for heating. Dom stopped at the hut of one of his men to see his very sick little boy. There was nothing he could do except offer kindness and sympathy. The little fellow did not make it, and soon five of his siblings died too. One of our best workers, a strong, handsome young man, only twenty, was working Saturday and by Tuesday he was dead. Zunico said, "It was probably pneumonia, as the Cholos catch that, and their treatment is to throw them in the icy river to cool their fever. They are not sick long after that. They are dead."

A procession came through the ranch. A mother, a father, a very young husband and four relatives bore a stretcher with the young wife, almost dead. They had walked for days and were headed for Cajamarca. Good gosh. I was constantly frantic about my children and broken hearted about all the others.

Then there was a fellow with a compound fracture of his ankle that for a week had been treated by plastering leaves on it and singing songs of magic. They asked El Doctor Dom for the only remedy they knew. Aspirin! Despair grabbed me yet again, but Dom said that in a week he would probably be bounding up and down the Andes again. Or dead. Funerals were occasions of joy, as they believed they would go straight to Heaven, and there was no doubt it had to be better than where they were. So they sang and danced, played their haunting music on their panpipes and their little harps, beat their drums and feasted until the corpse turned green. Then they would say that what really killed him was something he ate that turned him green. They drank a lot of "chi chi," a potent brew made of agave, their purple potatoes, and colored corn. Zunico told us all this.

Dom came back from Chile, telling of an amazing adventure. He had been directed to the hacienda of the Irrazurize family, fabulously rich Basques whose ancestors had been premiers of the country. (I just read that an Irrazurize was active in a Chilean uproar of some kind. They are still there!) He brought pictures of himself dressed in a dramatic, black Chilean poncho, leather chaps and a flat, black hat sitting on a fine horse with a fringed saddle blanket, bridle and breast collar. He was splendidly dashing! The parties, with important dignitaries, must have been glorious, and Dom felt he had served our country well in fostering good relationships.

He consulted on breeding programs, marketing strategies and parasite control. Parasites cost millions in Latin America, as they were endemic and made raising livestock very difficult. There was a 20% death loss across the continent from parasites, and in the two years Dom worked there, he was able to cut that significantly.

Little Pete's birthday was coming. There was no way to get a present for him so I took a big piece of eucalyptus firewood and carved a swell little boat. It even had a proud sail of scrap material. Elaine and I baked another amazing cake, and the party was on. Pete was delighted with his boat and took it to our pond to launch it, his Cholo friends eagerly watching. It sank! The green, dense wood just would not float. He had some choice comments about his stupid mother the lousy ship builder, but he liked the cake.

Dom's homecomings were passionate affairs, and once again I became pregnant. At that time, there wasn't anything to effectively prevent pregnancy, especially since it took only a gleaming glance my way from the dangerous Basque to knock me up, to put it bluntly. Blanca was also pregnant. Pedro moved her to relatives on the coast, explaining to Dom that at such high altitudes women other than Indians miscarried or had difficult pregnancies, dangerous deliveries, and often babies afflicted with birth defects. No medical care was available. Dom told me firmly that I was not to be "an ugly, sissy, American tourista," and that I was to have the baby at the Granja, with an Indian midwife, like everyone else there. Except Blanca. I was terrified, and as Blanca predicted, I began having "Soroche," high altitude sickness. One day I lay down on the children's bottom bunk and watched the bedspread above shake with my loud heartbeats. Elaine, only six, became a heroine, which she has largely remained all her life. She took care of her little siblings, she cooked and singed her bangs and eyebrows starting the stove and fireplace as I lay on the floor gasping and faint. It was pretty bad.

Pedro and Zunico came to dinner one evening. I managed to cook and serve, but as we sat down to eat, my left side, head to toe, went numb. Everything looked as though I was peering through water. Sounds grew farther and farther away. My tongue went numb. I

255

lay down on the couch, and in front of our guests, Dom began berating me, accusing me of being an ugly American-tourist-spoiled brat.

When I could get up again, I picked up a 12" cast iron frying pan and bashed him over the head with it. He got his arm up just in time to save his skull. His watch was shattered, his arm bruised from hand to elbow. Thank God he was so quick, as I might have killed him. Our guests scurried to the door. He did not speak for two weeks, which was a great relief. What revenge would he take? All seemed quiet for a while, like a volcano that just smokes. Then I understood about rage. Well I knew how it could blind one, even a nice one like me, and how horrible things can happen. The experience gave me compassion, even for me. I was not sorry. That man had it coming.

Pete developed a mass in his lower abdomen. Palpating it, I thought it might be a Wilm's tumor, a fatal cancer children develop. He couldn't straighten up, and walked around bent double. I wrote a frantic note and gave it to one of our workers saying, "El Patron. El Patron." Dom was a two-day's ride away at the eastern end of the Granja, dipping sheep for parasites in the jungle and he never received my plea for help. He came home five days later and instructed me to give Pete castor oil, which I was too smart to do. Zunico, alarmed for us, fired up the radio to the head office in Lima, and they ordered Dom to get Pete out of there.

Our jeep, our only transportation had been broken down for months, so Dom rode all night through the rain on his big grey horse, twenty-five miles to Cajamarca, to meet the twice-weekly plane to

Lima. The little plane was beginning to taxi out as he galloped after it, yelling and waving his poncho. He let the horse go and leaped in the cargo door, grabbed by someone inside. Zunico, who had ridden through the night with him, caught the horse and rode home to tell me about it. It took another week for Dom to get a truck and drive it back to the ranch to get us. Meanwhile, Soroche and all, I had managed to pack everything the children and I could take. Dom would later sell the furniture, books, and household items in Cajamarca at a surprising profit.

The truck bumped and skidded us to the airport, and once again we boarded the little plane, barely cleared the ridges and made it to Trujillo, a big commercial port city on the way to Lima. We had a long layover before the flight to Lima so Dom took us to the city to shop. He put little Paul on his shoulders, took Elaine's hand, and disappeared into the teeming crowd of Indians, leaving me with Pete, doubled painfully over, and baby Anne to attend to. I had no money, could speak very little Spanish, and must have looked alarming to all, for people skirted around us with worried stares. Not knowing what else to do, I walked along, hoping to find someone who spoke English. A Guardian angel came to help. Far up a side street I caught a glimpse of little Paul's head above the crowd, on his Dad's shoulders. We found them in a shop on a side street. I said nothing as I was afraid Dom had some awful plot to lose us. Maybe he was getting even for the bash on the head. What made me think I would get away with that, unavenged? I was in shock. I was afraid he had lost his mind, his behavior seemed so irresponsible.

He frequently talked about a beautiful Basque widow who owned a large estancia near Piura, north of Lima. He had spent considerable time there "helping" her, and he made no attempt to hide his admiration and affection for her. He said that if he were not already married, he would marry her. It made horrifying sense. His plan to have me deliver the baby with an Indian midwife and his total disregard for Pete's terrible lump and cystic fibrosis was murderous. He was ashamed that any child of his would be weak in any way, so ashamed of Pete he may have wished him gone. He blamed me for Pete's, and Jack's CF, unable to face such imperfection in himself. Both parents must carry the recessive gene that causes it, and he insisted it was only logical that if I had not carried it, his sons would be strong and healthy.

Somehow we made it to the plane and to Lima. The Simon Bolivar Hotel, Lima's finest at the time, seemed like a port in a bad storm, and we gratefully settled into a suite where we could have room service. We rarely saw Dom, but he did take Pete to a Peruvian government doctor, who, in alarm, scheduled us quickly on a flight back to the USA. Dom took us out to the plane, gave us each a peck on the cheek, turned and walked across the tarmac to the Limatambo terminal. He didn't even look back, and I thought we would never see him again. I couldn't help sobbing, while the children, alarmed and sad, patted me and began to cry too. The stewardess brought hot chocolate. We flew away.

The kindness of strangers helped us home. A couple from Santos, Brazil were flying to see their grandchildren in El Paso, Texas, and were eager to "practice" on my little tribe. Their kindness was a blessing. The children beguiled, or perhaps terrified Braniff personnel, and they stashed us in first class in the front of the plane. A convention of surgical supply salesmen asked me to join them playing poker. I had learned to play well enough on Remuda so that I rarely either lost or won much, and jokes brought merriment enough so that it turned out to be a pretty good party. Laughter heals, and fear about Pete and despair over Dom receded to tolerable levels. One of the salesmen was a wonderful young man who was going to Phoenix to join his wife and their seventeen-month-old child. In spite of his cool glamour, he took us under his wing and actually looked pleased when several people complimented him on his lovely family. I urged him to bring his wife and baby to Remuda, but he never did.

People seemed astonished that we were coming all the way from Peru, and I confess the kids and I enjoyed our short time of being amazing. And I was amazed and grateful for how kind everyone was, other than airline personnel who were truly frightened by us and with whom I battled constantly to get what we needed.

One sad thing happened. Little Paul, The Terrible Tempered Mr. Bang, lost his beloved little teddy bear in the Houston airport. His desperate distress alarmed me. That little bear seemed to be the focus of all his other losses, especially what he feared was the loss of his dad. I did all I could to find it, calling security, begging janitors to look, but he was nowhere to be found. It was a red flag, a warning that Paul was deeply wounded by the loss of his father and our traumatic move.

Top: The Avenida Nicolás de Piérola in Lima. Luxury time in Peru would be limited. Right: Elaine, Pete and Paul in the main square of Cajamarca, the nearest town to the Echeverria family residence on the Granja.

Opposite page, top: The Catholic church in Cajamarca where the Echeverrias attended mass. Bottom: Sophie holds baby Anne. The family posed for a picture en route to mass in Cajamarca. Atahualpa, the last great Inca Ruler, was imprisoned by the Spanish in Cajamarca.

Top: A typical Cholo home on Granja Porcon. Right: A Cholo riding the range.

Opposite page, top: Herders display Romeny Marsh lambs in the high corderos region of Granja Porcon. Bottom left: Dom castrates a sheep with his teeth. Bottom right: Peruvians on Granja Porcon drive horses in a circle to thresh grain.

Top: To celebrate Elaine's sixth birthday, the author made a cake out of ground corn-meal, sugar and cocoa. The Indian children in the background patiently waited for a slice.

Right: Maria holds her daughter. Maria was Sophie's friend and helper on the Granja.

GOOD GRIEF, HOME AGAIN

The Echeverrias wanted nothing to do with us, but they reluctantly took us in as we had no place to go. Remuda had no room until after the holidays. Paul was distraught and cried most of each night, even though he slept with me and I did all I could to comfort him. Pete was sick the entire time we were there, moaning and crying. Anne had been named "the traveler" as she would get her little arms and legs going like a little bear and off she would zoom, getting away from my harassed attention and into mischief. One of the last nights we were there Paul cried all night. He finally quieted down at five, just as "the traveler" awoke. I dashed down stairs with her, hoping she would not ruin the final few hours of sleep for her grandparents. And what did greet my wondering eyes in the living room, but Grandma and Grandpa sitting there, fully clothed, reading. I gasped and said weakly, "Couldn't you sleep?"

"No," they growled. I said, "Should we kill the children now or later? Grandma replied, "Now is as good a time as any." Thank God, Remuda found a room for us.

My family was not happy about taking us in either. We would need a room that could be used for paying guests and a lot of expensive food would go down our hatches. But take us in they did, putting us in a room they couldn't have rented anyway.

The room was in the back of Sophie's house, the one that used to be "Mother-in-Law Mansion." The ranch provided care for the children while I took Pete to Children's Hospital, in Denver, the place most qualified to address his problems.

Pete was subjected to many scary and painful tests and treatments. Back then parents were not allowed to stay with their children, as they were thought to cause trouble and confusion. I returned to the hospital the morning after some awful tests and found Pete crying piteously for a drink. I got him one, picked him up and left, nurses chasing us yelling that I couldn't do that. I replied," The hell I can't!" and I took him home. The lump had been extracted, and he was essentially all right, though it took years to heal the posttraumatic stress he suffered. Perhaps it never healed.

Dr. Robinson was the head of Children's Hospital. I obtained an appointment and confronted her with what turned out to be a powerful little speech, one of those times when that fierce Angel steps in with good words. In essence, the Angel and I told her that stress is a major factor in illness and to foster healing it must be addressed. Nothing could be more stressful to sick children than to be snatched from their parents and taken off to a strange and terrifying place to suffer God only knew what. Parents can be taught quickly how to be helpful rather than in the way, and must be permitted to be with their little people. Amazingly, good Dr. Robinson heard me, the rule was lifted, and provisions were made for parents to stay. Reclining chairs to sleep in were even provided. I love to think that I had a part in changing that cruel and destructive practice. Let it be known that, yes, we can bring about great good if we will get in there and DO it.

Pete and I returned to Remuda. I began having labor pains. Guardian angels again swooped in for us. Luis Salcedo was working in the lettuce fields west of Wickenburg, and was critically injured when a piece of farm machinery malfunctioned. He was hospitalized in Wickenburg, and his sister, Sitas, was summoned from her job as housekeeper for a wealthy family in California. She needed part-time work, and she found us, or we found her, and she saved our lives. Lovely, bright and kind, way over qualified for a group like ours, she took care of my little family while I lay in bed trying not to have my baby four months early.

My godparents, Jane and Ed Havey, used to stay at Remuda from opening day, October 1, to closing day May 1. They were a wonderful part of our lives, as they loved us three little Burden urchins, knew how to show it, and our times with them were vitally important. Little kids need to feel loved, and they provided that for us while our parents were busy running the ranch. Now here they were again, their love and kindness bolstering me up during that difficult time. Every evening they joined me in that ugly, dark room, and served up gin and tonics. How delicious, how welcome those drinks were! None of us knew pregnant women were not supposed to drink, and fortunately, I did not like to feel the effects of alcohol beyond a little lift of spirit. David, the baby I was trying so hard not to have early, turned out to be just fine. They say that what happens during pregnancy profoundly affects children, and I wonder if all that happened somehow explains the fire in Dave. He can be scary, but he is so brilliant he controls it and uses it wisely. We owe tremendous gratitude to the Haveys for giving us four and a half months of unconditional love, spiritual direction, guidance, peace, and all the fun we could stand.

Elaine was enrolled in first grade in Wickenburg's McClennan school, and as bright and delightful as she was, she was able to make friends and catch up. Pete and Paul were terrorizing the ranch, but fortunately there was plenty of open space and the dust they kicked up was not too destructive. Little Annie enchanted everyone.

On April 20, I began labor, right on time. We had made it. The new hospital in town had just been finished, and the old one was converted into the jail, except for a delivery table and one room in the old maternity wing. David was born in the Wickenburg jail, a real distinction, as no one else in town had such an entrance to this world.

The delivery was a difficult breech, and had we been in Peru, we both would have died. But we were not, thanks to God, Pete's lump which got us out of Peru, and Zunico, and we did well.

It was thought that cystic fibrosis may have been exacerbated by malnutrition in the mother. Since our diet was strange in Peru, and I had no access to vitamins, I ate everything I could. While hoping to get the nourishment the baby needed, I gained forty pounds. Dom lost all interest in me that last month or so in Peru. He treated me with the same disdain he showed for all fat, ugly women. Fortunately, Sitas took care of the children, making it possible for me to swim thirty laps every morning in the ranch pool and soon the fat melted away. Sitas and the kids joined me often, and they all learned to swim. She also made it possible for me to take them riding when there were enough horses left in the remuda, after the guests had been mounted. We called the rides, which included Annie and assorted small guest kids, "horse pulls" as we led, or pulled, gentle horses along with little folk squealing with delight on top. Elaine was a beautiful rider, admired and loved by the cowboys. Pete and Paul were wild, capable of riding alone, looking like peanuts up on their horses, but quick and capable. We explored all my favorite places and recreated many of the adventures my brothers and I had so relished when we were growing up. It was a very good time, and in six months I was in such good shape the cowboys were chasing me. Two of them took me to a party with dancing in Wickenburg. I thought as long as there were two, I was not committing sin, cheating on Dom, and I had a grand time until they wanted to really commit some sin. I escaped.

Pete was doing surprisingly well and his doctors urged me to keep him in Arizona, warm and benevolent, with low altitude that was obviously good for him. But they were also concerned about our separation from Dom and hoped he would soon return. Pete was probably not going to be around very long, and Dom should have as much time as possible with him. I said nothing, but the sad memory of Dom's disdain for Pete made me wonder if he would want to spend time with him at all. The kind doctors also believed Dom and I would need each other's support. Again I said nothing, but the idea that Dom might support me was painfully unlikely. I allowed myself to hope. The thought of taking Pete, and all of us, back to Granja Porcon was terrifying and our doctors were horrified at the prospect.

Dom was having a glorious time. The widow in Piura frequently needed his help, he was sent to many fascinating places on assignment, his mission was impressively successful, and the Point Four Program was begging him to sign a four-year contract. He spent little time at the Granja, but when he did, he had Zunico and the Cholos, all of whom loved him, to keep him company. He had essentially become a Peruvian. He also had Trapito, our ridiculous little cat, and a coati mundi he adored. Everyone loved those little animals, they were well cared for when Dom was away, and later, when he left for the United States he knew they would have good homes.

On a trip to Iquitos on the Amazon, Indians had given him the little coati mundi, small, furry, and full of mischief and fun. The Indians in the jungle on the Amazon were different from our Quechuas, larger, not as attractive, and they wore almost no clothes. No wonder, as it is a miserable area, hot and humid. But Dom had a way with just about everyone, and connections were made. The little coati was dashing around the house on the Granja one evening, jumping joyfully from couch to chair to table, when suddenly he just keeled over dead. Dom wrote that he was brokenhearted, and felt terrible guilt, because the tropics were home to his little friend, and the altitude caused what surely was a heart attack.

Dom seemed to be drifting away from us. He refused to send more than $150 a month, which did not even cover Pete's medicine. I was completely dependent on my family, who made it clear they were not happy with us. To make it up to them, I worked as hard as I physically could, with Sitas' taking care of the children. When the ranch closed in May, and the main crew left, I took over cooking for the seventeen or so people still living there. Cooking was never my thing, but by golly I got in that big, commercial kitchen and I learned how to turn out large meals that were good. I did not see it at the time, but it was training for the years to come.

The gardener was off for the summer, so I did the irrigating necessary to keep the ranch trees and shrubs alive. The kids helped with that, irrigating a lot more than the trees, merrily squirting each other with the hoses.

Sitas's brother had recovered, and she had returned to her much nicer, more lucrative job in Santa Barbara. Somehow we struggled through. I did not fit in at all with the people on the ranch that summer, who were trying to be "just too damned cool." One day I said something I thought was funny. They snickered and said, "Oh, that rapier wit!" A rapier was aimed right at my heart, then, and as often as they could.

The Echeverrias were disgusted with me. I had made the terrible mistake, hoping for her help, of telling Dom's mother that Dom seemed to be having an affair in Peru. She fired off both barrels at me, "What did you expect? You left him, you deserted him, you coward! So what if Pete died down there? He was going to die anyway! It is all your fault!"

What saved me was my wonderful children. What fun we had, swimming in the sparkling ranch pool, playing in the Hassayampa where it flowed through beautiful Box Canyon, playing ping pong, pool, and rummy, like I had when I was a child.

Thank goodness, summer ended and the ranch opened in the fall. John and Dana took Elaine, Pete and Paul to town every chance they got, and they sometimes broke away from entertaining guests to come up to our house to play with them. Al, our great old chef, cooked special dishes, even with all the cooking he had to do for the ranch, for Pete's needs. People were kind. Without their kindness we would not have survived, so forever I am grateful.

At first Elaine and Pete were rough with the guest children. Little Pete picked fights that he could not possibly win, and Elaine set up howls when kids gave her some of her own medicine after she had bullied them. They were Dom's children, and it seemed unfair that they were suffering unpopularity because of that Basque contentiousness. I worked hard to teach them how to get along better, and

272

in a short time they were doing well. Paul, the Terrible Tempered Mr. Bang, strangely, was not like them. He played wonderfully, right in the middle of everything, without hurting or being hurt by anyone. He called himself "boy nice," and indeed he was. Elaine became the queen of the ranch, with two little guest boys quite mad for her, but she did not trouble with these young swains, as her heart was true to Dave Smith, one of our cowboys on whom she had a huge crush. She also became a performer. At a Christmas party she stood on a chair and sang, acapella, "Silent Night" and "Jingle Bells" several times, and then she announced, "Now I will sing a song I wrote myself, 'Oh roll down your nose and curl up your toes, you are going to die tonight!'" She brought down the house.

Elaine, Pete, and Paul often cried for their dad. I showed them pictures of him and told them he would be with us again someday. One night Pete said the lights of Wickenburg were Limatambo, and he saw Dom's plane, and then Dom. He insisted he could see him, so I asked how he looked. "Fine. But he is not coming home yet. He is just standing there."

Pete continued to produce lumps in his abdomen. They seem to have been a nasty side effect of the artificial enzymes prescribed to replace the natural ones cystics cannot produce. Lumps formed in his intestines, and we faced an ongoing battle to get them to slip on through. A return to the hospital in Denver was a terrifying thought.

Along with the lumps, the little guy complained of feeling dizzy, and he said, "My legs are so tired." Pete talked about how he was going to die and how his guardian angel would take him up to Heaven. I listened and encouraged him to share his feelings and thoughts. My hope was to make Heaven seem real and wonderful to him, but he already seemed to know. Whatever I might add would be superfluous. Children who are very ill are often remarkable that way. Their sense of wonder and their connection to the Higher Power is clear and strong, eclipsing our own understanding.

My mom asked me what I hoped the new baby would be, and I said, "A little boy." She looked surprised and asked, "Why? You already have Pete and Paul." I explained that we would not get to keep little Pete. She said, "I suspected as much. We must keep it a secret." She did not know what he had, but I was glad I had talked to her about it as I hoped she would be a support for me. But she couldn't be, really, as she had to run the ranch. Alone, I turned more fervently to the Higher Power. Getting to Mass in Wickenburg was nearly impossible as I had no car, but praying and "listening" kept me afloat. Cousin Bud James finally found me an old, green Dodge sedan for $300. Yeah! No longer did I have to beg to borrow ranch cars for essential trips to town.

Every year Wickenburg held Gold Rush Days, a fine, noisy celebration of all that is western. A big parade is part of it, and everyone wanted the little Echeverrias on the ranch float. Elaine was dressed as the outlaw Black Bart, with big mustache and two six-guns. Pete was a drunk Mexican and played the part so well we wondered where he had learned that sort of thing. As they went by, people clapped and

Pete enthusiastically clapped right back. Paul rode in the truck with all the littlest ranch kids. They were a hit! I watched, laughing, from the sidelines with little Anne and baby Dave.

So it was, and always had been, our ability to "have fun anyway" and "to keep laughing no matter how happy we are" that carried us through. We savored and celebrated all the delightful things we could do. And the people who caused pain? In my lady-like way, joined by my small children, scandalously we would say, "F-k all those folk! Open some beer and jump in the pool!"

Dom had a change of heart, or sanity, and began wooing me with seductive love letters. I was swept away again by that darkly irresistible man. I didn't know what to think. Maybe the Basque widow in Piura had dumped him. I just hung on, not letting anything get me down and having fun. Warily, but with excitement, I waited to see "what was next."

Here Came Dom! Look Out!

Dom had taken a cargo steamer from Lima's port, Callao, up the coast, through the Panama Canal and the Caribbean, and on to New York. Obviously, he was not that eager to get back to us. He said it was probably his only chance to do that, and the two week trip was, in his words, "Wonderful." He spent time in New York, then in Washington D.C., debriefing with the heads of the Point Four Program. Finally he boarded a plane for Phoenix.

John, Dana, and Mom drove the children and me to the Phoenix Airport. A large plane taxied up, and the stairway was put in place. Dom descended in a Stetson, ostrich skin boots, tan gabardine pants, a white shirt and tweed jacket, stunningly handsome. He walked toward us radiating assurance and prestige. He was a man to be held in awe, an exotic presence that vibrantly filled his space on Earth. There was a hesitancy in his greeting, and in mine. A quick peck on a cheek was all either of us could manage. Elaine and Pete remembered him well, even after we had been apart for fourteen months, and greeted him with hugs and kisses. Little Paul, always very much his own man, observed with wary curiosity. But tiny Anne, just two, and David, under a year old, were terrified, and began crying and clinging to me. Dom was shocked and furious. He never really got over that, and carried animosity and even hatred for those two little people the rest of his life. He told me he would never forgive them for screaming in terror at him, wonderful him, in spite of my pleas, and in spite of recognizing that they were just babies. It was strange, and tragic, and, I thought, sick.

His magnetism swept over me, even so. As soon as we arrived back at Remuda, we went to the storeroom under the Kettering building to stash his luggage. Some mattresses were stored there, and our seventh child, Sophie Dominik was conceived in a rush of passion, forgiveness, and a New Beginning.

NEXT STOP, COLORADO

Obviously the Burdens wanted me and mine out of their hair, and Dom wanted to start our new lives away from there just as much. We left the children at Remuda, in the reluctant care of the Burdens and the ranch staff, and flew to Denver, drove to Longmont, and looked at all the homes that were for sale as fast as we could. Longmont was the town of choice as it was more or less centrally located for the ranches and farms Dom planned to lease for the sheep. I liked it because it was only forty miles from Denver, where the University of Colorado Medical Center was located with its excellent staff and facility for treating cystic fibrosis. Just as important, though not as urgent, it afforded symphonies, ballets, operas, plays and museums. I loved the arts and was determined that my children would be blessed with access to the beauty that would light up their lives and help them become all they could be.

The house we found was on a corner, with two lots, so, Dom said, "I can park trucks and trailers up and down both sides of the property." How might that endear us to our new neighbors? Hopefully they would hardly notice. It was on the east side of town, less prestigious then the west, where the golf course and the big homes were, so we would not be constrained by neighbors who lived according to propriety and status. We were prescient, as neither propriety nor status was in our destiny, and had we been among Longmont's elite, we would have driven them mad.

The house was solid, brick, and boringly plain, but it had room, light, trees, and a wonderful, big yard. We were told there were about fifty-two young children in the two blocks around us. St. John's Catholic School was five minutes away. We bought it, flew back to Arizona, collected our little tribe, and left Remuda.

Dom had arranged for his brothers, also sheep ranchers, to care for our best bands of outstanding Montana ewes while we were in Peru. He retrieved them, shipped them north and began pasturing them on the leased lands around our area. Dom's brothers were probably sad to have them go as they had produced well for them.

The sheep cleaned up what was left after crops had been harvested, provided their particular brand of fertilizer and broke and aerated the land with their sharp little hooves. They also loved weeds. The farmers loved them, and Dom. He established a reputation for honesty and square dealing, and was so well liked that he was told by several, "I don't have to count your bands when you come on my land. I trust your numbers."

The children and I unpacked and moved in. One morning I was

working like a doggoned dog, hauling the luggage and the treasures Dom had brought back from Peru, and stashing or arranging them "appropriately," I hoped. The treasures included some beautiful furniture topped in bull leather intricately carved with art depicting Inca culture and legends. There were juacos, Peruvian pottery that also depicted ancient cultures, and a lot of elegant silver. One of the first things I did was have one wall of the living room made into handsome bookshelves to house our treasured library and Peruvian art. It was coming along well when one of our neighbors across the street came running in, yelling, Mrs. Echermania (our name was next to impossible to pronounce for many), "Your son! Your son!" There was little Paul, two-and-a-half years old, stark naked, peeing off the garage roof, laughing merrily. I got him down, and dressed, but it was plain to the neighborhood that there was to be excitement at 119 Eleventh Avenue.

The fifty-two kids soon found us, and our little home became the center for fun, except when Dom came home. The kids were terrified of him, and small wonder. He breezed in, a powerhouse, with trucks, with Basques from Spain, and full of purpose and no nonsense. Everyone knew his truck, and when the kids heard it coming the call went out, "He's coming! Let's get out of here!" Our children, equally alarmed, dashed around picking messes up and looking as industrious and studious as they could. He usually greeted us all with hugs and questions about how we were, then he sank into the couch to read--he was a voracious reader---and demanded, "SHUT UP," or "AUS-HALIK," which is Basque for shut up. I cooked.

On February 17, 1959, little Sophie Dominik joined us, in the old Longmont Hospital, at cocktail hour. Dr. Haley and Dom left immediately after her birth to celebrate. My mother managed to leave Remuda and fly to Longmont to help us, bless her heart. She made it to all the births except Anne's, which came three weeks early. Remuda suffered her absence, and she could not stay more than ten days, which surely was fortunate for her, as we were "uncivilized" in her view, and chaotic. Her time with us made her work at Remuda look easier.

Basques don't tolerate food that isn't made from scratch, all fresh and natural. We always had good meat, usually twice a day, as any time a sheep looked like it was going to die, Dom shot it in the head, slit its throat, gutted it out, saved the hide, brought the carcass home and slung it on the kitchen table for me to cut up and cook. I never could stand the violence, and zoomed off to my "unreality," escaping to thoughts of lovely things, turning on fine music, and often having some wine, but the meat was excellent. I became so good at dealing with the carcasses I thought if all else failed, I could go to work in a supermarket meat department.

Elaine, Anne and I learned to make Basque sheepherder bread in great mounds of loaves, but we couldn't get it quite as good as the herders did. Dom said, "You just need a little sheep manure, like they have." As if that were not discouraging enough, the children loved it so much they would come home from school and devour a huge loaf, and then not have room for dinner. The same happened with cakes and cookies. They ate so much raw dough, and I have to admit I did too,

280

that what made it to dinner was pretty small. There had to be enough left for Dom and the assortment of men he had with him when they drifted in, usually late. The girls and I became expert at creating food that was "flexible," hot and fresh if they arrived on time, no matter how many of them there might be, but easy to keep if they were late.

"Star Trek" and "Gilligan's Island" saved us from disastrous dinners. We did not have TV until 1968, when Dom let me rent one for Winston Churchill's magnificent funeral and the Winter Olympics. He was quite taken with it and said I could buy one, oh JOY! I didn't allow much watching, and the children seemed to prefer reading and doing art, and of course their rowdy playing, but those chaotic hours before dinner were saved for me as they zoned out with Captain Kirk and Mr. Spock so I could cook. "Star Trek" hooked me too. The stories were essentially morality plays set in outer space, delightfully removed from reality, with characters ranging from outrageously righteous to gloriously bizarre, and I felt right at home.

Our boring, entirely too "American Suburban" house slowly morphed into a home that was really ours. We painted the doors purple, orange, red, green and bright blue and we papered a wall with a panoramic photo of a beach. Our carpet was the color of catsup and dirt, which, as hoped, didn't show the lively goings on. Over the years we had collected some lovely paintings, which livened up the plain walls. The kids painted one of their rooms the colors they loved. That room went from purple to blue to brown to red over the years, to the horror of our friends who happened to see it, but to the delight of the neighborhood kids. The boys' room was paneled in pine and escaped paint, but not thumbtack holes where posters and art went up. There were also some bullet holes. Dom taught us all to shoot and there were some close calls before the children understood the danger. Our guardian angels probably had grey hair and ulcers, or whatever angels get from extreme stress.

There was not enough money when it came time to paint the kitchen, so we just wrote wise and funny sayings all over it with Magic Markers. There was quite a diversity of quotes from Khalil Gibran to raunchy bumper-sticker eye-poppers and things we thought up ourselves. Instead of a proper kitchen it became a center of wonder, intellectually challenging and a source of laughter. Many of the neighborhood kids added their wit and wisdom.

Within that neighborhood were two families who became friends for life. Doctors Schmid and Amoroso and their wives, Jeannie and Joanne had moved in up the block in 1958, when we did. They bailed out and bought more elegant homes on the east side of town as soon as their practices made it possible, but the friendships between us and our children continue to this day.

We had a cement block wall built, just under the legal six-foot height, all around our big back yard, fencing us in and everyone else out. We painted it alternating primary colors so it looked nothing like a cement prison enclosure. A red concrete basketball and tennis court fit in the back corner, to the delight of the neighbors and the many friends the kids brought home from school.

The Rocky Mountain National Park had taken over and condemned the Stouffers' guest ranch, near Estes Park. The Stouffers were good friends who had been guests at Remuda. Their lovely lodge had been there practically forever, affording great vacations for people who loved being in the park. I went to the auction to commiserate, where the common response was that the park's action was outrageous. I ended up buying some doors, scrap lumber and tin roofing, which I hauled home to build a really swell play house in the backyard, under our biggest trees. Many happy times were spent there. Years later the children confessed that "Doctor" was a frequent game, but innocent me, how could I have known? With all those little people around, a lot got missed in the chaos.

Every Saturday, Longmont held a farmers' market and livestock sale. We bought produce and became proficient at finding "treasures" at the auction, like much needed sheets and cheap household stuff. One spring day there was a crate of fuzzy, yellow ducklings, so adorable I agreed to let the kids get a couple. Well, we couldn't leave their siblings there to fall prey to God knew what fate, so we ended up with a back yard full of little quackers. The boys dug a pond, somehow we convinced our cats and dogs to leave them alone, and there they were, peeping and quacking and pooping, to our delight and that of the neighborhood kids.

On June 3, 1962, Joseph Burden Echeverria was born in the brand new Longmont Hospital. He immediately exhibited the symptoms Jack and Pete had. How could it be? CF again. Dom had taken me to the delivery room and stayed until I produced, then he took one look and left. Dr. Haley had given me a shot to hurry it all up as it was cocktail hour and Dom and he had a tradition to keep. Dom did not come back, as he never did, afflicted as he was with his phobia about hospitals. When Joe and I were ready to go home, we called a taxi. Dr. Haley's wife, Maxine, happened in as I was calling and said, "What!!! Outrageous!" and she took us home in her Cadillac, a fine beginning I thought.

One Saturday there was, completely out of place, a baby grand piano among the Farmer's Market auction bargains. The bids stuck at $157, unbelievable! So I bought it. It took up a quarter of our living room, and no one played it, in spite of the teachers I hired. Pete could pound out tunes by ear, a remarkable talent, but eventually the kids persuaded me to trade it for a magnificent stereo set, which they could play very well.

We all loved music, from Jimi Hendrix and Janice Joplin to classical and everything in between. Jimi and Janis were troubling to me as they sounded like they were in agony, which I guess they were, but the kids "got" them. Pete was the only one who played an instrument. He became an impressive drummer, and the house shook on its foundations. I thought, "Good God, I'm going to lose my hearing!" Earplugs were out because meanwhile others were threatening murder and mayhem, and I did not want to miss any of that. Pete, so sick with CF, loved his drums and his music, so no way would I deny him that.

The girls sang in St. John's choir, or at least Elaine did. Anne and Sophie quickly bailed out of the nuns' discipline. Elaine still has a lovely voice, but Anne traded music for art. Sophie became a Flamenco dancer and singer and performs professionally from time to time. At one performance, she forgot the words to her song, which was in Spanish, of course. Looking down at her audience she thought, "They don't speak Spanish, so they will never know," and she followed in the footsteps of her grandfather Jack, and substituted "Achechona" and whatever came to mind. It worked quite well.

Dom probably had musical talent, unrecognized. He said that when he was at a party at the University of Iowa, he got up and sang "As Time Goes By." Hard as that was to believe, Dom never lied, so he must have been able to sing. He always hummed tunes from the classical music I played. He definitely had an ear for music.

DNA is just astounding, popping up time and again. Remember the tunnel John, Dana and I dug on Remuda Ranch that caused such a hooraw? Pete, Paul, Dave and Joe, with some help from their sisters, dug a fantastic tunnel that started under our house, went under the side lawn, under our neighbor Mrs. Seewald's fence and into her garden. Mrs. Seewald was a terror. She accused Paul of stealing her watermelons from under her refrigerator, pure insanity. She had no melons, they wouldn't fit under a refrigerator, and none of us had ever been in her house. The boys accidentally lobbed a ball from our ball court into her yard. She grabbed it, snarling, and would not give it back. Hence the tunnel. They broke surface amidst her glorious flowers, retrieved the ball, and dived back underground to escape.

Of course the neighborhood troops were enthralled, and they got together, gathered shovels and buckets and dug another spectacular tunnel in a vacant lot. As had happened back on Remuda, some overly cautious parent found out about it, and had it filled in. Damn. Creativity nipped in the bud once again.

The City of Longmont put in a new power line and placed a huge pole right on our corner. Pete was incensed. "What in hell makes them think they can put that hideous thing right in our yard?" he snorted. He grabbed an ax and chopped that hummer almost down before the neighbors called the police. Where was I? Who knows? Pete called me from the county jail in Boulder, where he had been taken, happy to shock my socks off, something he loved to do. I drove the twelve miles there and stamped into the jail, threatening to sue if they even thought of keeping Pete with his health problems. I am a gentle soul, rather shy, really, but when things get bad, I seem to have a guardian angel who is fierce and can get us out of all kinds of scrapes.

Jail doors clanged and out came the prisoner. As we drove out of Boulder, he said, "Damn it, Mom! You just ruined one of the most interesting experiences I have ever had!" He was mad. I made a quick U-turn and headed back to turn him over for a night among the drunks and druggies, but he said, "Oh, that's okay, you can take me home."

The grand piano was gone, and Pete decided we should have kept it. The Baptist Church, a few blocks away, kindly gave him permission to come play theirs anytime they were not using it. Pete had bought a bike from a friend, and pedaled over there late one night. The church was locked, but it was easy for him to break in and there he was, playing away, until here came the police again. Not only had he broken in, but his bike's ID had been filed off. It was hot, a stolen item, though Pete did not know that. Off to jail again, and off I went to post bail. That winter I spent so much time in court I got a book read while I sat in a back pew, as Pete and others, whom I kindly "don't recall," stood trial. Graffiti had been drawn on town sidewalks. There had been some "altercations." Thank God, we had managed to instill basic honesty and honor, and nothing they did was worse than mischief. I even found myself standing before "Hizz Honor" defending one of our dogs who had gone roaming. He fined me, lectured me, and I was free, and officially one of the "Echeverria Wild Bunch," as we came to be known.

DOM'S PHILOSOPHIES

Dom was terrifyingly worse than our obstreperous kids could ever dream of being. A manifestation of what we thought had to be his periodic insanity was the way he drove. Never did he come within ten miles an hour of a speed limit, and his speeding tickets piled high. He was even arrested for reading his mail while driving. Passing on curves, or on hills, or in traffic bothered him not at all, as he believed he was psychic and knew the road was clear. His favorite sayings echoed time and again. "When in doubt, step on the gas!" Or, "When you are going to break the law, look both ways first."

I lived in terror, especially when he had children with him. His psychic abilities failed him many times and a few of his crashes were serious. He had a phobia about hospitals, and would call me frantically saying, "Come get me out of here!" I would rescue him, take him home and plaster him up as best I could. He had charge accounts with the tow truck and the garage, as our trucks spent a lot of time there.

Twice his driver's license was revoked, the first time for a year, and the second for three. He hired a series of drivers who lived in our basement, but they could not stand the pace Dom set, and he ended up driving himself for those years. His Basque foremen had failed to get licenses, it was too difficult since they were in the country on special work permits, so there we were with a fleet of nine trucks, no driver's licenses, and no insurance.

Hernan Zunico, our great friend from Peru, had come to work for Dom. He was determined to get a driver's license, and was, like his boss, reading the pamphlet on how to do it as he drove a pickup truck down I- 75, the main freeway to Denver. The wind caught the pamphlet and when Zunico reached to save it the truck veered off the highway and crashed. Dom was following him, and was the first on the scene. Zunico was unconscious. Dom ran to his truck to speed to the nearest phone he could find (this was pre-cell phones) to call for an ambulance. He told me later that he was so in shock he found himself almost to Denver, unable to remember where he was going. By then others had stopped and an ambulance arrived to rush Zunico to the Longmont Hospital.

Dom's phobia about hospitals was so strong that after one look at his dear friend, lying unconscious in ICU, he ordered me to stay with him. By then we had found a marvelous woman who took care of the children, the house, and me. I called Monica, and left for the hospital. Zunico lived only a few days. He never regained consciousness. I talked to him and held his hand until he gave a loud snore and left us. The funeral was small and sad, with just the other herders and our family. Zunico is buried in Longmont.

Dom imported Basque relatives and a network of men from Spain. The Western Range Association had agreements with the federal government that permitted ranchers to bring over men who would do work that American men would not or could not do. They came on three-year contracts, and were required to return to Spain, or Peru, for three months at the end of their contracts. The Basques saved every penny they earned, never went to town, ordered minimal personal supplies, and went home to Spain with fists full of dollars.

Dom believed it was best to have his foremen close, so they lived in our basement, two to five at a time. Dom's cousins, Poli and Juan Oroz, and Dom's most valued assistant, Jose Marie Artaecheverria, were part of the family. How valuable my experience cooking on Remuda turned out to be! Elaine, Anne, and I had to crank out meals for the whole crew.

They were not the only ones we fed. They brought us all the little lambs that were orphaned, and we bottle fed the beloved little "bums" until they were big enough to go back out to the bands. When it was too cold for them, we kept them on our enclosed back porch, bedded with straw to make them comfortable and to soak up anything that needed to be soaked up. A sheep panel kept them out of the kitchen, mostly. We raised a batch of twenty-eight which we sold for enough money to buy a dishwasher. Dom had forbidden that, saying, "You have Elaine and Anne, for goodness sake." But the bums were ours, the money was ours, hallelujah! For once, Dom's mother was on our side and said, in her rich, lively accent, "You get one that is built in, when he is not around, so he can't make you take it back." And so we did.

One happy day Dom brought home five bushels of gorgeous peaches, and ordered me to can them. Out came the cookbook, but it said nothing about not running the peels through the disposal. Peach skins started to bubble up through the basement plumbing, flooding the whole place. It took three men to haul the soaked, ruined carpet out to the trash barrels, and all of us (except Dom) to clean it up. I was fearful Dom would never speak to me again, but the neat, shiny rows of preserved peaches and the fine jams were so wonderful, all was forgiven.

Emma YaYa was a young Peruvian woman Dom brought to this country to help me. Maybe she and Zunico were more than just fellow Peruvians, but we never knew. Emma was a "caution." Peruvian girls are programmed from birth to please men. Their little ears are pierced and ear studs inserted in the hospital when they are born, and from then on it is all about being beautiful and seductive. Emma had been trained as a seamstress, and in this she was useful to us, but mostly her energy went toward being beautiful and seductive. Work? What was I, La Senora, supposed to be doing? Finally, one day, when I asked her to do something she blew up and accused me of abusing her. Back to Peru with you, honey. Some of the herders surely missed her.

Dom had loaded a two-ton truck with fine rams to breed the

bands of ewes we were pasturing in western Colorado. Paul and Elaine rode with him while I followed in the station wagon with the rest of the family. Independence Pass is winding and steep, and there Dom went, careening down it full speed. Paul said he was terrified, which is saying a lot, as "The Terrible Tempered Mr. Bang" was usually fearless. Tires screeched at every turn, and the rams staggered back and forth threatening to fall and suffocate each other as sheep do when they pile up. I was terrified too, trying to keep up, but we could not catch the big truck. Disaster seemed inevitable. Elaine, Paul and many thousands of dollars worth of rams were surely headed for death, along with Dom. Paul said, "Dad had a look of evil glee on his face. He was grinning!" Meanwhile, the girls, Dave, Joe and I prayed. We were heard, as somehow we leveled off safely on the flat highway below the pass. None of us dared to ask Dom what in the world he was thinking, nor could we imagine what it might have been.

When he was working a summer job between his two years at the University of Colorado, he had done almost the same thing. His job was driving a tour bus through the Rocky Mountain National Park, with its steeply winding roads that top out at over 10,500 feet. A tour group made up of elderly people began to complain that he was taking the curves too fast. Infuriated, he stepped on the gas, careened down the highway, his passengers screaming as they flailed about, until he pulled up at the station. He got out and walked away, knowing he would be fired and there would be no pay-check. He was so proud of that day he told the story for years.

What was it with him? My grandmother, mother, and a dear friend, Nancy Chase came visiting. We drove them up into Rocky Mountain National Park, Dom at the wheel, and they began to look terrified. I begged Dom to slow down for them, which infuriated him. He left the highway and sped across a long, steep meadow, sliding on the grass, and screeching to a halt at the lip of a precipice that dropped into a glacial lake. We were so scared we were almost physically ill. He just laughed, backed up, took us to Estes Park and bought us dinner. Of course, as always, he was wonderfully charming. Waitresses, stewardesses, and any women who came near, twitched and twinkled at him. How could someone so dreadful be so engaging and nice?

The police rang the doorbell one afternoon. They had come to arrest Dr. Echeverria. If he were put in jail, how would I manage all our sheep? That fierce guardian angel stepped up and lied through my teeth to the officers. I was amazed at how smooth and how convincing that angel was. Dom, hiding in a closet, escaped. The priest who heard my confession allowed as how the angel knew best, and I got off with three Hail Marys.

The University of Iowa, where Dom had been a student as a Navy Air Force cadet, contacted him—he was well known as a prominent sheep man—asking him to host their entire college of agriculture and animal husbandry so that they could see a real ranch operation. We had leased a beautiful ranch on the west side of LaVeta Pass in southern Colorado, and several thousand of our sheep were grazing there. Dom planned a Basque welcome for the college, so the herders, the children and I cooked paella, Echenique cake, sheep herder bread and other delectables. The herders and Dom castrated (docked is the term used by ranchers) all the lambs the morning the university students were to arrive. "Juavitos" is a specialty, the testicles cooked in large, cast iron skillets over camp fires with olive oil and garlic. We roasted legs of lamb and the feast was sure to be splendid. Two Greyhound buses pulled up to the campsite and out poured the students. Dom toured them around the bands of sheep, told them how it all worked, and then we served the feast. They did not know what the juavitos were until after they had eaten them and they were exclaiming about how good they were. Shocked is what those young men were, but they rolled with it and were delighted. They loaded up and drove away.

Dom left in his pickup. He had the keys to my station wagon in his pocket as he had used it to show some students around. There the children and I were, alone in the cold, on the edge of a dark forest. The herders had gone off to their camps. Terror crept in as we remembered that just the week before a family from Denver was camping on La Veta Pass, and a bear had dragged one of their children, screaming, from the tent, never to be seen again. Bears love garbage. There was plenty lying around. We all got in the station wagon and prayed. At two in the morning, it occurred to Dom that he should probably check on us and we were rescued.

The bears proved a terrible problem. They ate so many sheep we realized no profit, so that was the end of the lease on that splendid ranch.

A ranch was for sale near Ely, Nevada, and Dom was interested in buying it. Large enough to accommodate most of our sheep and cattle, he thought we could end our gypsy ways and stay in one place. Nevada was good ranch country, and it had a large population of Basques. We left the children with Monica Barela and drove to Ely, checked into a Basque hotel, and had dinner. The next morning we were to tour the ranch. Dom said, after dinner, "You go on up to the room. I know you hate gambling, but I want to check out the casino here in the hotel." At one o'clock in the morning, he came in. He looked pale and distressed. "What happened?" I asked. He looked down, paused, and said, "I can see that I could become addicted to gambling. It almost got me. We can't be here where I would be tempted all the time. We are going home first thing in the morning." Admiration and love filled me as we drove away. What insight and courage he had!

Dom was away so much with our sheep and he was under such pressure that when he finally came home, conversations were brief and mostly about business. The children were getting wilder and neither I nor the priests, nor the good sisters, were having much luck with control. Earnest talks with Dom about needing him to be a father and spend time with us went nowhere. He snorted and replied, "Mary has raised her five children without any help from Mike, and they are a lot better and a lot nicer than your kids." He used to say, "The only people who have problems are stupid idiots!" We learned never to tell him anything that was not wonderful and cleverly we perfected skills for hiding pain and problems from him.

Mary was the lovely Basque Dom had wanted to marry, but whom his brother Mike had captured while Dom was in the Navy Air Corps. There was no doubt that she had a hard life. Mike was a foul-mouthed, cheating alcoholic and a profligate gambler. As the oldest son, his father had put him at the head of their extensive sheep and cattle business. Mike gambled away fortunes of the company money until finally his younger brothers convinced their father to turn it over to them. Mike took off for Texas, leaving Mary and the children behind. He somehow survived. Maybe the mistress he had was rich. Dom's concern for Mary, shared by all of us, was deep and sad.

She was a strong, bright woman and the children she raised alone were indeed wonderful, but with the wisdom of years, looking back, mine were easily as good if perhaps more "colorful." Comparisons are odious anyway. She found support and guidance in her devotion to the Catholic church and community, just as I did. The church, the priests, the nuns, and our fellow parishioners were supportive and kind. I clung to them, as she did, like someone drowning hangs on to an inner tube.

We must have been something of a mission for them. The nuns called me from time to time saying, "Sophie, you must do something! Little Sophie is a heretic and a rebel!" Or, "Sophie, you must do something! Your sons beat up "so and so"!"—although "so and so" usually had it coming, I found.

Much as I appreciated and loved the people in St. John's, I had trouble with Catholicism. Converted when I began having children so that I would be in unison with Dom, who was Catholic, and to honor the bargain I had ridiculously made with God when Jack was born, I had not been able to buy the whole pie. Secretly I was proud of little Soph, and of her equally "free thinking" (but not as outspoken) siblings, and of her brothers for addressing wrongs on the playground, but to my friends the nuns I just replied, "Oh dear."

No matter these little problems, I was enlisted to teach Catholic education to the parish high school students. Surely something was learned, but after about a year, I was FIRED! For heresy! I was so proud—one of my best days. I had suggested that the church gravely underestimated God. The ineffably grand and glorious Force that permeates all, and from whom all is created, cannot be so small, so petty, so cruel that babies, or anyone who has not been sloshed in the baptismal font is denied His, or Her presence in Heaven, wherever that may be. What is more, I told them, God, Yahweh, Krishna, whatever name you want, must love all He creates and no soul will be lost, even if 10,000 reincarnations are needed for some, like Hitler, to get it right. There must be dark to juxtapose against light, and somehow the Divine Dance arranges it in time. Our free will, without which we could not grow or take credit for achievement, is always honored, but if we use it unwisely we get unending chances in reincarnations. No wonder I was fired. Fervently, I hope my students took some of it in.

The priests invited me to lunch at the rectory from time to time. I was a partially converted convert who had read the lives of just about all the Saints, including St. Thomas Aquinas' *Summa Theological*, some of which I understood. I could argue for hours with those learned men and since I had many grains of salt to offer, there was laughter. What a mission it became to straighten the Echeverrias out! Those kind men supplied for me, and somewhat for the children, the masculine influence and emotional support that Dom was too busy to give us.

Dom was, in fact, so absent that one night when he turned up for a school play starring some of our children, Sister Johnita exclaimed, "Good Heavens! He does exist! We thought the children were just dreaming him up so they would have a Dad like everyone else."

Dom was not to be blamed. He was running a livestock enterprise that grew from our meager start with 246 old ewes, to one of the ten largest sheep operations in the nation. One year he was given the largest wool incentive payment in history. The wool incentive was a government program to aid sheep producers who had to compete with imports, and it was based on wool produced. The program was financed through taxation of wool and lamb imports. To have reached the top of that list was quite an accomplishment.

We were proud to be his partners and glad to help all we could but it was an unusual and difficult life. Friends were mystified and asked me why I tolerated what they perceived as the abandonment of me and of his parental role. I tried to explain that we were business partners, and that his role was the most difficult. It demanded long hours, hard work, much travel in all kinds of weather, and he needed all the help I could give him. They could not quite understand. Some of their children began to get it as we took them to help us with loading or unloading trains and trucks and driving bands of thousands to pastures. Shearing, branding, docking, and especially lambing amazed them. Excitement and adventure beyond their imaginations were ours, and we gained quite a following of youngsters who loved it.

One time, and one time only, I tried to confide in Joanne and Jeannie about the pain Dom inflicted. They both replied, "How can you say anything against that wonderful man! You are so blessed to be his wife!" His violence, his cruelty and his craziness somehow stayed hidden from them. So be it. We enjoyed his wonderful reputation. He was a man to be proud of.

THE ETCHEPARES AND CYSTIC FIBROSIS

Paul Etchepare was a lamb buyer for Swift and Company when Dom first met him. Paul, a French Basque, was married to lovely, blonde Hellen, who had been an English teacher, well educated and elegant. They had five children, bright and lively with some "colorful" issues, though not quite as outrageous as ours, lucky them. They had the advantage that Paul was fully involved in their lives. Hellen did not have to work, had full-time help, was wiser than I, and seemed to be a much better mother. The Etchepare children had lovely manners and were civilized. We learned much from them. They learned a lot from us, too. Two of their sons spent summers with us as it was hoped that working for Dom would change some teenage behaviors that were out of control. Like smoking and drinking. Maybe it worked. They grew up to be wonderful men. Our two families had so much in common we became life-long friends. Gratitude for that is profound and eternal.

They lived in Denver, in a fine, large home on Seventeenth and Hudson, one of the city's nicest neighborhoods. Hellen and I shared a delight in Denver cultural events to which we took our children. My mother used to say it was important for families to "Slop up culture like hogs," so that is what we did. The Museum of Natural History, The Denver Zoo and the Denver Art Museum were frequent hangouts. Dom actually joined us for some of the concerts and plays that we loved. He fell asleep and snored through the great Spanish guitarist, Andres Segovia's concert. The children giggled. I relied on my ability to dissociate and to hear and see only what I wanted, so his snores did not bother me. Some have accused me of not paying attention and even of being spacey, but at the same time, they envied me for my cheery joy, so there. Staying out of touch with reality is a useful survival skill, though it might have been better if I had rolled up a program and whacked him on the head.

Since we lived in Colorado, by God, we were going to ski. That is what Colorado is about. We could not afford to do it as elegantly as the Etchepare children and some of our other friends did, but we managed. We made picnic lunches and thermoses of cocoa, arrived at the slopes in time to eat and grab the half-day lift tickets, which made it affordable for seven children and me. In time we skied almost all the areas in Colorado.

After a lesson or two, I could slide down the slope pretty well, until one day a teenager fell near me, breaking both legs. Horrible! Then I heard of a doctor and his wife who joined a long lift line. She said she had to go to the bathroom, but he insisted she stick it out so they wouldn't lose their place in line, and he assured her, "You can go at the top. There is surely a restroom up there." Well, there was not, so she skied down into some trees, undid everything and relieved her desperation, but as she stood up, her skis did that thing they sometimes do. They just took off, and down the slope she went, struggling to get her pants back up, which she finally did. Next morning at breakfast a young man hobbled in with bandages and crutches. "What happened to you?" he was asked. "Well, yesterday I was skiing along when this lady whizzed past with her pants around her ankles, and I ran into a tree." I retired from downhill and took up cross-country skiing and snowshoeing, which are much less dangerous. My children, undaunted, kept right on zooming down hill.

It's hard to recognize one's family watching skiers come down the slopes. Bundled up, they all look alike, but soon I could tell mine. They always schussed down crouched like racers, passing everyone, no turns, and caught air alarmingly. Sometimes they crashed. Paul learned to do impressive flips off moguls, but one time he bounced after the first flip and landed on his head, breaking his neck. He said, "I knew it was broken, I could hear it crack, and I was seeing stars." So what did he do? He handed his poles to his friend so he could hold his neck up, and skied on down to the First Aid Station. Later he needed surgery to fuse the breaks, a dreadful procedure in which the doctor went through the front of his throat to shore up his spine. It still hurts, many years later, but it has not slowed him down, and he still skis, but no flips.

There were other bang-ups. One Christmas season the boys headed up to a ski shop on "The Hill" near the University in Boulder to buy gifts. I needed to ask them something so I called the shop, saying, "I would like to speak to one of my sons. You can tell them as one has a broken leg and the other a broken neck." "They are here," was the reply. Maybe they were there, but were they all here?

Beautiful, young Toni Etchepare was being trained for Colorado's entry in the Winter Olympics as a downhill racer, when a reporter jumped out in front of her to get a picture for the Denver Post. She veered to miss him, crashed into a tree and suffered a concussion so severe we were terrified she would never be normal again. For about a year she could not be left alone, as she was so confused she wandered off and couldn't take care of herself. Hellen, a saint if ever there was one, coped. Eventually Toni came out of it and married well, and has been a force for good in Wyoming politics. God is good.

The Battle is Joined

The Etchepares were among the founders of the Colorado Chapter of the National Cystic Fibrosis Foundation, because of our sons. Amazingly, guests of Remuda Ranch, Ben and Bess McCabe had a grandson, Benjy, who had CF and it was said they founded the very first chapter of the National Cystic Fibrosis Foundation. God is not only good, he is weird. How strangely entwined we all are, whether we see it or not.

Dom joined us in our projects, and we did some remarkable

fund raising. Paul Etchepare donated one of his excellent Warren Livestock Quarter Horse fillies to be auctioned off. Dom, our youngest son Joe—who was small and adorable—and I were in newspaper articles, holding the horse, looking good. Hundreds of thousands were raised. We secured the Grand Opening of the Denver Playboy Club, a spectacular event and another large pile of money went to CF research. Joe, at five years old, was the Poster Boy for CF. He appeared in the Denver Post and the Rocky Mountain News with Marilyn, a bodacious Bunny whom we all loved, she was so sweet. Later, Joe confessed he was a little bothered by her "dumplings, which were boiling over," as Bunnies' dumplings always are.

Denver provided a pool of generous people who participated in casino nights, receptions, theatrical events and luncheons in the best country clubs and restaurants, including the famous Brown Palace. The CF Board was meeting in the Presidential Suite, and when we finished, I left to go down to the Ship Room, where we had spent many happy times over the years. There was an escalator that descended from the mezzanine and down I went, headed for a merry gathering there. A little group of priests was milling around on the landing. Suddenly they looked my way and began crossing themselves, horrified looks on their faces. "WHAT?" I thought. Have I forgotten some important garment, like my skirt? It was not I. Whizzing past me, down the median strip between the up and down stairs, came my little sons. The priests caught them as they landed; I thanked them and said some prayers of my own.

The CF chapter elected me Vice President. There were meetings, trips to establish a chapter in Wyoming, and much exciting and productive activity. The children endured horrible babysitters while I worked, and I felt anxiety and guilt, but sly and imaginative, they often out smarted those women. We had good neighbors, and the police department who knew us all too well, that they could call. Eventually, the teenagers became so difficult, and with Dom's Basque foremen living in the basement, ladies, nice or not, would no longer babysit. However, some of Longmont's off duty policemen would. Years later, the boys confessed that they used to give the cops some beer, sit them down in front of the TV, and go to the basement and raise hell. Well, by the grace of that weird God, we all survived. When there is something like CF, or any dreadful condition, you just long to be able to do SOMETHING, and that was my "something," so I continued to serve no matter childcare problems. It also gave me an outlet to life beyond Longmont and some valuable friends.

Research was being conducted at the University of Colorado Medical Center in Denver, and Pete, Joe and I were asked to participate. As a carrier of the defective gene, I revealed some weird little symptoms, and later I could see them in some of my children indicating that they too might be carriers. Through research, a test to identify carriers is now available, and my children faced the dilemma as they married, to know or not to know. They asked, "Would you have had children if you had known?" I replied, "Absolutely. As painful and difficult as it has been, we were blessed by the presence of Jack, Pete and Joe. I would send no one back." Pete interjected when he heard that, "Well, I wish to hell I had never been born!" God, how many knives have to be stuck in our hearts?

Ernest Becker wrote *The Denial of Death*, in which he addresses such dark and dreary issues. Here is one to ruin your day:

"Creation is a nightmare spectacular taking place on a planet that has been soaked for hundreds of millions of years in the blood of all its creatures. I think that taking life seriously means something like this: that whatever man does on this planet has to be done in the lived truth of the terror of creation, of the grotesque, of the rumble of panic beneath everything. Otherwise it is false. Whatever is achieved must be achieved with the full exercise of passion, of vision, of pain, of fear, and of sorrow. How do we know that our part of the meaning of the universe might not be a rhythm in sorrow? Life seeks to expand in an unknown direction for unknown reasons. There is a driving force behind a mystery that we cannot understand and it includes more than reason alone. The urge to cosmic heroism, then, is sacred and mysterious, and not to be neatly ordered and rationalized by science and secularism."

Actually, my day is not ruined at all. Deepak Chopra M.D, that remarkable mystic, said (I paraphrase) that if something is known, etched in granite, you are stuck, but where there is uncertainty, anything is possible. That is exciting, especially since there is so much about which I am uncertain, including Pete's declaration of wishing he had never been born and Becker's view of our bloody planet. Therein lies the mystery, stretching before us to infinity. How can hope be denied? So, if we become unstuck, blessed with uncertainty, we can think whatever we want.

The psychiatric department at the University Medical Center asked me to talk to the entire department about how it is to parent cystics. My phobia about speaking to more than a group of friends nearly sank me, but I found a chair behind a small table so no one could see my skirt hem shaking. They asked how I handled the guilt of carrying the fatal gene. "For God's sake, I am no more guilty than my sons are of having it," I exclaimed. What a dumb question! Then I remembered how Dom said it was entirely my fault. He could not face the fact that he had a part in it. I spared the doctors that. They wanted to know how I had managed to provide the boys with the fun and the "devil be damned" attitude that seemed so beneficial.

Good heavens, what was going on with these guys? We, the boys and I, took care of medical stuff such as mist tents, nebulizers, respiratory therapy and hands full of pills as fast and unnoticeably as possible, rarely saying much about any of it. Then, fun! Adventure! Work, which afforded real self worth! What would be more sensible? They seemed to expect a more grave and serious approach. I left a little unsettled, but later in the elevator one of the doctors said, "You handled yourself extremely well, Mrs. Echeverria." What a relief! I hoped I had struck a blow for wiser ways to approach life for stricken children.

Pete and I were asked to help create some kind of counseling program to help families cope with cystic children who were living longer. Cystics used to die before they reached school age, and by the time we were asked to help, some, like Pete, lived into their teens, but CF is always fatal, and that creates despair, anger, depression and sometimes episodes of psychosis. We met with a group of parents and patients at the University hospital. It was awful. Sadly, Pete felt bad about the children who were sicker than he was, and was equally upset that he wasn't as well as the ones who were better. No one wanted to talk about it. The parents seemed offended that I refused to bend to the gravity of the illness. So that was the end of that.

Top photo: Pete riding on Remuda Ranch. Bottom left: Paul, "the Terrible Tempered Mr. Bang," with a baby burro. Bottom right: Sitas Salcedo. The author writes, "After returning from Peru, Sitas 'saved our lives' by providing much needed help with the children."

Opposite page, top: Sophie shares her saddle with Paul on a ride up Box Canyon, a favorite desitnation. Pete is on the horse in front. Bottom left: Anne at Remuda Ranch, 1958. Bottom right: Paul and Pete, dressed for dinner at Remuda after returning from Peru, 1958.

This page, top: The Echeverria family, circa 1960. L to R Sophie, holding baby Sophie, David, Paul, Elaine. Pete, Anne and Dom. Bottom left: Sophie, age 2.

Top photo: Sophie and her children, decked out in their Basque berets, before boarding the Durango-Silverton Train. Joe was yet to be born. L to R: David, Paul, Sophie Dominik, Anne, Pete and Elaine. Right: Sophie and Dom on a business trip to Denver, early 1960s.

Opposite page, top: Pete, Paul and Dom riding horses, early 1960s. Bottom left: David's kindergarten picture. Bottom right: "Cowboy Joe," taken in Longmont circa 1963.

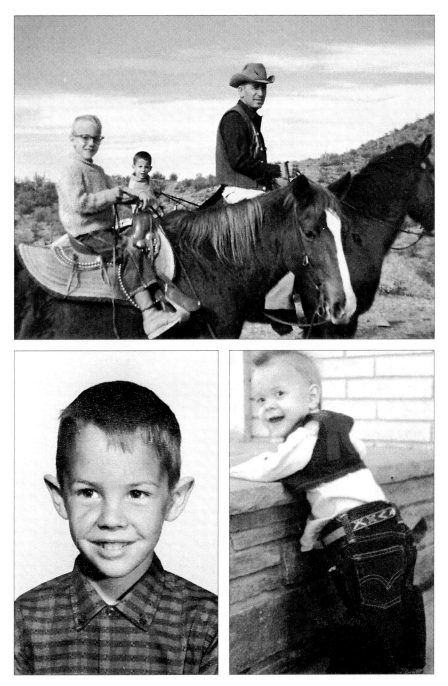

Opposite page, top: Paul rides a corralled sheep in Wyoming, circa 1964. Bottom: Sophie Dominik and Anne, great little cowgirls!

This page, top: The Echeverria family. Picture was taken in the backyard of their Longmont, Colorado, home in 1964. L to R: Dom, Joe with lamb, Sophie Dominik, Sophie, Paul, Anne, Pete and David. Elaine, not pictured, was at St. Gertrude's Catholic School in Boulder. Left: An orphan lamb, or "bum," follows Joe.

Top: Joe poses in Longmont with rare quintuplet lambs, 1967. Right: Joe, age 5, holds a Quarter Horse filly Paul Etchepare donated to raise funds for the Colorado Chapter of the Cystic Fibrosis Foundation. Joe was named Colorado's 1967 Cystic Fibrosis Poster Boy.

316

This page: A bunny with a bunny. Joe was given a bunny by Playboy Bunny Marilyn Mason to promote the opening of the new Denver Playboy Club. The November 1967 opening served as a fund raising event for the Colorado Chapter of the Cystic Fibrosis Foundation. The author, pictured right, looks on.

THE SHEEP RANCHERS GATHER

Every year the Wool Growers and the Lamb Feeders Associations held conventions. They were grand events where we gathered at some fine venue or other, the men to rant and rail over business, we ladies to shop, eat, and relish time out from being livestock wives. I loved those times. The women were interesting, strong and bright, always providing wisdom about who we were and how our roles could be best served. Las Vegas was one of the places we gathered. At a splendid dinner we were sitting around a big table feasting and drinking when the ladies suddenly looked aghast while our men practically cheered. Down from the ceiling came golden cages in which gorgeous naked women stood seductively. They were astonishing all right, but I thought the horrified looks on my friends were more amazing.

One evening we gathered in a bar where Don Rickles, a famous comedian was doing his schtick. Rickles's humor was based on insult and derision and he saw us livestock folk as fine fodder. After a few volleys, we all looked at each other, nodded, and got up and walked out, leaving Rickles stewing. The cool thing would have been to parry his nastiness and just laugh, but we had the courage not to buy into it. Good for us!

We livestock people were kind of discombobulated in "Lost Wages." There is no daytime there in the hotels with their darkened casinos. The men gambled. The women shopped, or gambled. I put fifteen nickels in a slot machine and did not win a thing and I am still mad. So I went swimming in the hotel pool where the sun was shining. It was good to leave, but I was grateful for the fun, such as it was.

Phoenix, Portland and San Francisco were much better. The husbands had their meetings, the ladies shopped. Since shopping is not my favorite thing, I went exploring and got lost in San Francisco, wandering around down by the docks, eating Ghirardelli chocolate, and coming face to face with the gay community. What a revelation they were, flitting about flaunting their "identities" in somewhat obscene ways. There were no taxis, which should have been a red flag, but BART, the public transport, would surely get me back, I hoped, so I hopped on. Damn, you needed tokens! A hippie with a wild, red Afro rescued me, proving yet again that kindness is everywhere if you project open acceptance and friendliness, or, as in my case, if you are a dumb blonde adrift in their city.

A PRINCESS IN OUR MIDST

Elaine, lovely and bright, was Dom's princess. He sent her to Mount Saint Gertrude's Academy in Boulder after she graduated from St. John's grammar school, so that she would advance in her faith and be safe from all that might threaten her, like boys. One of the most valuable experiences in my life had been Lincoln School, in Rhode Island, and I prevailed upon Dom to send her there for her last two years. She was a boarder, with a roommate who remained her dear friend for many years. Penny Guy was American, but she had grown up in "Calli in the Valley," in Venezuela, where her father did something in the oil industry. Other students were just as interesting, and Elaine was equally so to them, westerner that she was. Her beautiful voice won her a place in the Lamberquins, the Lincoln Glee Club, who sang in several languages and a number of disciplines, all classical, of course. She also starred in school theatricals, as I had—there is the DNA again—but she was Madam Butterfly while I had just been Nell by whom right was not done. (The play I was in was "He Ain't Done Right By Nell.") She had a Jewish boyfriend, Gary Misch, who was so serious about her that he grilled her about CF, and how in peril their children might be. Elaine and I were taken aback, to put it mildly. It had not occurred to us that this would be an issue in her courtships.

Dom and I flew to her graduation. How lovely she was, and how proud we were! The girls, all in white, long dresses, carried bouquets of white flowers and paraded across the school lawn to be awarded their diplomas and to be praised by Miss Schaffner, the splendid woman who had succeeded beloved Miss Cole who had been so important to me.

Prescott College came next. There was an orientation during which the freshmen had to scale a local mountain, Thumb Butte, and then rappel down. Elaine's rope broke and she dangled upside down until she somehow scrambled around for a spare line. Then kayaking on Lake Powell was required where she was caught in a whirlpool and nearly did not escape. With fervent prayers, she suddenly shot out. The last of orientation was a three-day solo during which each student had only string, a pocketknife and a journal. The intent was to put the young students in touch with their inner beings or something. What Elaine got in touch with was hallucinations from hunger. She reported that it was quite interesting, though terrifying, and she was proud to have survived. The college took many pictures of her and she graced the cover of the college brochure and an article inside, looking ethereally lovely, but hungry and dazed. A year of Prescott and she had had enough.

She transferred to The College of Santa Fe, run by the Christian Brothers, where we were sure there would be none of the laissez faire influence that permeated Prescott, and where she would be protected in her Catholic faith. Her first night there she called us to ask what to do with her roommate, who was falling down drunk. Good Heavens! Put her in the shower, give her some coffee was all I could think of. Brother Joseph, head of the college, loved Elaine. They became fast friends until he died. His guidance, however, did not protect her from falling in love with Billy Fellers, the son of wealthy Texans. Therein lies another tale, another adventure, another tragedy. But for now, back to the chaos of our lively life in lovely Longmont.

Dom leased pastures and ranges for the sheep in New Mexico, Kansas, and Wyoming as well as Colorado. During the school year, we stayed home while he traveled. We took care of the sheep around Longmont, often unloading triple-decker cars in railroad yards. Dom would call, saying, "Two cars are coming in. Get the kids out of school, unload the sheep and trail them up to Sekich's," or whatever farm he had leased. The nuns and priests were fascinated and let us miss school. Of course we had to take care of the herders too, shopping for provisions at the Corner Pantry for them. Paul was an excellent shopper and often took over for me. The owners, the Schopbachs, liked us. Thank goodness. One day they called and said, "Sophie, you left one of your children here." Little Sophie was immersed in comic books, which they displayed on a bottom shelf, bless their hearts, just for little people like Soph. There was so much noise and activity that I just didn't notice she was not among us. How awful! But the Schopbachs seemed to be amused and took good care of her until I could speed back. My son Paul has said Sophie was not the only one I forgot, but I do not remember. God and everyone else, please forgive me!

When summer rolled around and school was out, we followed our sheep wherever Dom had pasture. Our funny little dog, Mayi, had her puppies in the LaBonte Hotel in Douglas, Wyoming, so one of them was named LaBonte. We drifted over to Big Hollow, west of Laramie, a vast expanse of good grass. After the sheep were unloaded from the trucks and the herder's camp was set up, we went to town where Dom crammed us into rooms at the Conner Hotel. We cleaned up and went to dinner in the hotel dining room. The children, tired and hungry, dared to be a little noisy. Dom gave me some money, ordered me to take them all to the greasy spoon dump across the street. Golly Moses, how shaming, how painful it was, but it was better than what he usually did when anyone displayed bad manners. He would poke them in the head with his fork, sometimes drawing blood. Of course Elaine, his favorite, dined with him at the hotel.

We stayed in all the worst hotels in Wyoming and New Mexico, but we did not mind, as they were only beds and bathrooms. Sometimes they were what one might call educational. Once the children ran up to me saying, "Mommy, the prostitutes are in the rooms across the hall from us!" They gathered knowledge none of their friends in dear old St. Johns School had. But the sheep, the wild ranges and the gorgeous scenery were what mattered most.

THE QUARTER CIRCLE 5 RANCHES

The Schwabacher family owned The Quarter Circle 5 Ranches west of Pinedale in northern Wyoming. They were cattle people, but the Bureau of Land Management wanted them to graze sheep, also, as the combination is excellent, in spite of myths to the contrary. Sheep eat weeds, noxious and pesky for cattle, if they are put on the ranges in early spring. Their fertilizer is excellent, and their little hooves aerate land auspiciously. Then the cattle follow them in, eating the higher grasses the sheep don't like. They even do well grazing together. The Schwabachers knew nothing about sheep and were glad Dom came along with his bands of thousands. They were unloaded from trucks and trailed up into the Schwabacher Sections, a beautiful, gentle range of hills crowned with Aspen groves and meadows. Wyoming Wagon sheep camps were pulled up into the groves. Often the herders would fire up their little camp stoves and make us strong coffee with sugar and canned milk. Starbucks, eat your heart out.

As summer came, the sections began to dry out and we trailed the bands up into higher, greener country. There was a bridge over the Green River that served as a gate into the grazing permits on the Forest Service land held by the Schwabachers. As they raced across the bridge, rangers counted the sheep to insure Forest Service restrictions on grazing numbers were met. Their counts were never as good as Dom's, who was a genius at it. Truckers and the rangers used to bet him. They couldn't believe how he could count so fast, by groups, ten, twenty, and then when he hit a hundred, he would shout "YO!" and one of us would switch a pebble from one hand to another. He won money, a Stetson hat, and lots of swell prizes, and we enjoyed his fame.

Motorized vehicles were prohibited, so our Wyoming Wagons, their arched roofs covered in canvas, their interiors so efficient a man could live there comfortably, were pulled by great draft horses loaned from the Quarter Circle 5, the home ranch. The country was wild! Over the summer the herders shot the bears, cougars and coyotes that hoped to feast on our sheep, and we gathered a collection of their hides and heads. It was forbidden, but it was so remote the rangers did not catch us.

Dom, never one to bother with rules, "looked both ways" and loaded us up in his little blue Ford Bronco and across that bridge we went, high up into the forests. Streams sparkled among rocks and we waded and explored. We tried to collect the marvelous fossils of fish, ferns and shells that we found, but they were set in granite. We visited the first camp near Rock Creek, making a list of the herder's needs, and then we headed up to the next permit, Tosi. A ewe was crippling along, not able to keep up with her band. Dom threw her in the back of the Bronco, which was already overloaded with groceries for the camps. He took Anne and Dave and tied them with one skinny rope to the hood of the Bronco. Terrified, I did all I could to get them back in the car no matter how crowded we would be, but it only made him angry. He retaliated by driving hell bent for election through the forest, over rocks, out onto a meadow that ended at the edge of huge cliff. He skidded to a stop at the very edge. I was afraid I would faint. Anne and Dave were dead silent, holding on to windshield wipers and that skinny rope for dear life. I wished Dom would go look over the edge of the cliff so we could push him over, but no such luck. Somehow we made it back down through the forest, Dave and Anne were now on the back bumper, clinging to whatever they could with their fingernails. Dave remembers sheer terror. The ewe was left with her band, now bedding down for the evening. Across the bridge and on to the Schwabacher's Quarter Circle 5 we went.

The ranch had two homes, one was a sleek, modern house for the Schwabachers, next to their little airfield where they parked their "his and her" airplanes. We were their guests in the splendid old mansion, which had been the summer home of a governor at one time. The Fourth of July brought friends from Longmont to celebrate with us. Dr. Chris and Joanne Amoroso and their five children arrived ready for celebration. Joanne, warmly, generously, Italian, cooked a glorious feast on the big, eight burner stove in the mansion's enormous kitchen. A pot was bubbling or sizzling on every burner when suddenly water began streaming out of the ceiling into every single pot! Joanne and I looked at each other in shock and horror. One of the children upstairs had been sick and flushed too much, stopping the plumbing up, and the overflow flowed. We opened some wine and segued to pizza they had packed in a cooler. And cake! Then fireworks! A fine time it was, in spite of the plumbing. We understood why the Schwabachers had fled the grand old place.

I had been so terrified and so angry at Dom for his insane behavior up on the permits that I wanted to kill him, but now we were having such a glorious time, such a grand adventure, making interesting friends like the delightful Schwabachers that my dark feelings were replaced with gratitude for what he made possible for us.

The Baca Grant

The Baca Grant north of Santa Fe, New Mexico, was an immense spread that had been deeded to Señor Baca by the Spanish Crown back in the colonial days. We were excited to be shipping two bands of sheep there, each consisting of from 1,200 to 2,000 sheep. How fine they looked as they unloaded onto the vast, green meadows! Dom's cousin Poli Oroz, from Spain, Dom's brother Bob, his wife, Bert, and their three children came to join us there for a wonderful picnic in that gorgeous country.

Baca Grant is in the wilderness west of Los Alamos, where the atom bomb was created. Los Alamos was pretty well buttoned down, and we had to be cleared at the entrance and were permitted to see very little. Talk was about the bomb, what it meant, and how tragic it was for one of its inventors, Robert Oppenheimer, who grieved about having created it for the rest of his life. One of our friends back in Longmont, Ray Bassett, had been in the crew on either the Enola Gay or its companion plane when Nagasaki was bombed and he would never speak about it. We sensed deep distress, even though he said he understood why it had to happen.

I took the children to Santa Fe and The Bishop's Lodge to see where their uncles and I had spent our three wondrous summers. It was much too expensive for us to stay there though we did have lunch in the big dining room with its beautiful murals. Back we went to Espanola and a motel easily as dreadful as all those hotels in Wyoming.

Summer ended, the sheep were shipped back to Colorado, and we returned to Longmont. We were so busy with the sheep that we had almost no social life. During our first years there, Dom and I were invited to many dinners. So often, he simply did not turn up and I arrived alone, that the invitations trailed off. When I invited friends to our house, the girls and I put on what we thought were really nice feasts. Again, Dom might or might not appear, and when he did he often fell asleep on the couch, but we managed to have fun anyway. Years later it got back to me that if you were invited to the Echeverria's you would have a fine, funny time and you could count on lamb, sheep herder

328

bread, Stouffer's spinach soufflé from the Corner Pantry's frozen food section, and Basque Echenique cake. Always. Well, doggone, that was the only menu we felt confident about. We were also known for our orphan lambs that frolicked around the yard unless it was snowing or raining, then they frolicked around the house amongst the elegant linens, silver, china and crystal we had received as wedding presents and had brought back from Peru. It all seemed fine to us. Oh well.

SCHOOLS

St. John's had no athletic program, so I enrolled the boys in ballet class with their sisters. Ballet is an excellent discipline; in fact football players sometimes take lessons to improve agility. The girls were lovely and talented. Pete, Paul, and Dave appeared for class in their black leotards, white socks and t-shirts. The teachers and the little girls were thrilled, as "men" are hard to come by in ballet. However, those three boys were so hysterically funny, trying their best to plié, entrechat, and all that swell French stuff, that everyone just broke up laughing. It became quite hopeless, and sadly we were asked to re-move those comical young dancers so classes could continue.

Paul and Dave tried to play basketball when they got to high school, but Dom needed them with the sheep so often they were not dependable and had to drop out. Pete was too ill. Scholastically they did well enough. Anne was brilliant. Pete was absent too often with his illness to do very well. Paul was so smart his friends often asked him to help with homework, but somehow, he began to slip. His grades went down, and absences were reported so often that I started driving him to the high school and watching him go in so I knew he was there. How innocent I was! He just went out the back door. His friends, all from nice families, found it beguiling, and Paul led Longmont youth down a bad road. But Dave was great, little Soph and Joe followed along behind their siblings and all was well enough, I thought. I hoped.

I provided all the cultural input I could. My friend Jeannie Schmid loved to tell of the time she visited, unannounced, and found lambs galloping around, cats and dogs on the furniture, baby Joe crawling around needing a change of diapers, while I read *The Owl and The Pussy Cat* to the rest of them, in French. Anyway we all thought it was probably French. Classical music was lending a strange ambiance to the scene. Jeannie said she loved visiting me because it gave her something to talk about for two weeks.

Top: Sophie Dominik, dressed for her First Communion. Joe, pictured to her right, is already a heretic! Right: Freshman Elaine in her St. Gertrude's uniform.

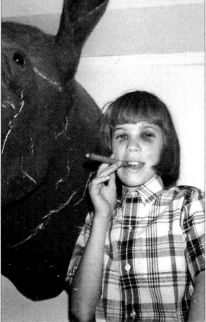

Top: Dom caught a sandhill crane chick at a Wyoming herding camp. The chick was not pleased and gave him a good peck. Anne laughs at the interaction. Around the same time, Anne had her own run-in with a horse while she was herding cattle. The result is shown to the left. The picture was taken at Schwabachers' Quarter Circle 5 Ranch. She posed next to their rhinoceros in parody of a cigarette ad campaign saying smokers would rather "fight than switch." Anne said she fought and switched to cigars.

Opposite page, top and lower left: A Wyoming Wagon Sheep camp. Lower right: Elaine, Pete, Paul and Anne play in a rock formation on the Lembke's beautiful ranch south of Laramie, Wyoming.

This page, top and right: The author hastily shot these photos of a frightened Anne and Dave after Dom loosely tied them to the hood of his Bronco. The children held on for dear life as Dom tore down rough terrain in the Gros Ventres. Writes the author: "I was terrified that this might be the LAST pictures I ever took of them." Dom's erratic behavior was a harbinger of things to come.

BLACK CLOUDS THREATEN

Celebration was becoming more difficult at 119 Eleventh Avenue. Pete's trips to the hospital became more frequent, and what we called "The Black Cloud" hovered over us, always threatening. Little Joe was just as ill. Dom, unable to face CF, was absent more frequently and when he did come home, he was troubled and tense.

He would ask me, "Do I look old?" Or, "Do you think I am fat?" "Heavens no!" I of course assured him, though naturally he was aging, and he had taken on a little ballast. Then he told me, "Go to a beauty parlor and get yourself fixed. You look old. You are getting wrinkles." I began dressing where he could not see me and I made sure my clothes covered as much of me as possible, night and day.

The best course of thought was to assume that he would never compromise our marriage vows in spite of my wrinkles. He had ample opportunity, he was away so much, and when he came home he often went on at length about the women he had met. "She cooked up a terrific chicken dinner for us in about twenty minutes!" "Just once before I die I would like to bounce around on top of some gal who had big boobs like so and so." The boys told me that the truck ran out of gas once on one of those lonesome Wyoming highways. Dom thumbed a ride with a red headed woman in a convertible. He left them to watch the truck, and he didn't return for four hours. Rock Springs was only thirty minutes away, and they wondered about that.

His rages escalated. He caught one of our kittens defecating and he picked it up, strangled it to death and threw it out in the gutter with the children watching and crying in horror. His abuse of sheep became uglier. If some poor, old ewe was reluctant to go up a chute into a truck, he would throw her on the ground and stamp on her, sometimes to death. He gouged out eyes, rammed sticks up vaginas, twisted ears, all the while yelling obscenities. We did all we could to maneuver any fractious animal that might infuriate him out of his way. We tried to get them to go up loading chutes or through counting gates so smoothly that he wouldn't get mad. When he did fly into one of those black rages and started beating some slow sheep or frightened lamb, I would shudder and keep silent. I never forgot the time I was yelling for him to stop torturing a ewe, and he yelled back, "You better be glad it is not you!"

He twisted arms, smacked heads, stuck forks in scalps if manners offended him; he kicked us and yelled insults, even at me, in front of the Basque herders. He never hit me, though he did twist my arms. He lifted little Dave up by his ears and Dave was deaf for two weeks. Dom forbade me to take him to a doctor. I frantically prayed for him to go out to the sheep so I could take Dave for help. Suddenly Dave could hear again, thank God. Paul remembers being picked up by his ears so violently he heard them crack as they separated from his skull. I managed to get him to a doctor who gave him penicillin shots for two weeks. Doctors, by law, are now required to report child abuse like that, but back then, nothing at all was said.

The Half Moon Motel in Pinedale, Wyoming, was often our home when we had sheep in the area. An attractive, blonde widow with big breasts and a bright mind ran it. Dom used to put the children and me in our rooms and tell us to stay there, saying he would "be back later." Later is when he would get back. Much later. I concentrated on the great times we had had that day, driving sheep up to gorgeous ranches, and my mind zeroed in on our tomorrows, when we would again be out in our beloved Wyoming having adventures. Our lives were truly wonderful. There was so much for which to be grateful. I could be truly grateful for Dom Echeverria. He caused great pain, but he also brought incredible joy. As with most men who abuse, he followed his outbursts with beguiling behavior. Presents! Perfume! Wild, irresistible passion! And always the excitement of our adventurous lives.

The Black Cloud of cystic fibrosis hovered. The children lurched into their teens. I went to a beauty parlor. Several men other than Dom seemed to think it worked well. At a Wool Grower's banquet, a colleague asked me to dance, and whispered to me that I was beautiful. I danced on, then and later, metaphorically, relishing that affirmation.

I gained strength, and stood up for us more and more. Driving home from Rawlins one day, Dom began railing at Pete who had dared to ask to drive. "You sickly weakling! You are worthless," he snarled. Without thinking I whammed him across the mouth with the back of my hand, and commanded him to turn the truck over to Pete. He shut up, got out of the truck and Pete was our driver. The kids were silent, but joy could be felt. Another time Dom began swearing at me, calling me a stupid idiot, and I whacked him over the head with a frying pan again, as I had in Peru, breaking another watch and bruising his arm to the elbow. I demanded that he should never, ever talk to me like that again, but I wondered when the next time would be. He was scary and out of control.

Sometimes, when Dom was over the top, out of bounds, seemingly crazy, I would wonder what I was doing, hanging in there, failing to rescue us. The lovely belief that our friendship and our love was profound and that we were, in some Holy way, helping each other to become the people God intended us to be, began to seem utterly ridiculous. What an illusion I had been entertaining! There was fear he would escalate into really dangerous behavior. The responsible action might be to take the children, the kittens, the dogs, and whatever else was in harms way, trust in God, and GO. But there was no way we could survive without our sheep. CF is horrendously expensive to treat. There were so many of us, all deserving, needing, good schooling, college, and of course food, shelter and decent clothes. Those days of the past when we survived on garage sales would not suffice now. The sheep, the sheep, we had to have our sheep. Without Dom, it would be impossible. I also feared that if we left, it might precipitate even worse violence.

Nightmares plagued me. Then day would break, the sun would shine, and gratitude for so much that was ours would take over. There was something about my children and me that lifted us out of the muck and the darkness, and we just went on. People often asked me how we did it, and the only answer I could give was that we had humor, often pretty black, and we were able to laugh. There was great love. The grander thing we had was faith. We knew our angels were with us, or how else could we possibly still be alive? And the Force was with us. I often asked myself, "What next?" Who knew? We would laugh, and "when in doubt we would step on the gas." We would not only survive, we would transcend. Unless we did not…

Epilogue

We were sliding into a deep, dark hole. Who wants to read or write about deep holes?

BUT, the Force was with us and an astonishing event turned us around! A new book is in the works, titled with another of Dr. Dom Echeverria's "wise" sayings: *When You Are Going To Break The Law, Look Both Ways First.* While we were no longer slithering towards disaster, life was still tumultuous. The next book will be as full of our "confusions" and adventures as the first. If you choose not to dive into it, please be at peace. We are all right, those of us who have survived. Unless we are not.

To be notified when Part II of Sophie's memoir,

When you are Going to Break the Law, Look Both Ways First,

is released, please email sophnano@gmail.com.